"Unless the Lord builds the house,
the builders labor in vain."
Psalms 127:1

ELEMENTS: A STATEMENT OF
FUNDAMENTAL PRINCIPLES OR FACTS.

THE
ELEMENTS
OF
BUILDING

A Business Handbook For
Residential Builders & Tradesmen

MARK Q. KERSON

Every effort has been made to provide correct phone numbers
and internet addresses, however neither the publisher nor the
author assumes any responsibly for errors in this information,
third party sites, or changes that occur after publication.

Printed in the United States of America

First Edition, 2014
Second Printing

ISBN 978-0-9913277-0-6

From The Ground Up Publishing
2401 A 28th St
Santa Monica, CA 90405

Book design by Six Penny Graphics, VA

Edited by Guy Maynard, OR

Index by Cole Freelance Indexing, MO

for Lisa

life is infinitely better because of your

deep awareness

gentle heart

and those lovely green eyes

TABLE OF CONTENTS

INTRODUCTION

As a young carpenter-builder I searched long and hard for useful advice about the non-construction aspects of residential building: how to manage money, deal with customers, use professionals, hire and manage employees and subs, and much more. Either I did not find it at all or I found it scattered in bits and pieces, thus most of my answers came by trial and error: a slow, confusing, and often painful process. Throughout my career I met hundreds of tradesmen and builders who, often without realizing it, were looking for the same information that I was. Therefore, this book is written for myself 30+ years ago, and for the painter-plumber-drywaller-carpenter—for the tradesman—who, having mastered a craft, determine to open a business.

The idea for this book came while working as a carpenter and going to college where I discovered *The Elements of Style* by Strunk & White. The book explained English composition succinctly in a manner I could both understand and use. As it says in the introduction, the authors "…cut the vast tangle of English rhetoric down to size and write its rules and principles on the head of a pin." It provided rules, but more importantly it discussed nuance and possibilities and almost from the moment I discovered it I imagined finding a similar book for residential construction. Like its namesake it would provide rules and the more elusive information required to establish and run a construction business. I envisioned a small book, well worn, which, like a seasoned builder, offered encouragement and advice gleaned from years of experience.

I never found such a book, but I held onto the idea throughout my career and kept notebooks of mistakes made,

1

lessons learned, solutions found, advice received, and the best of the books and articles I found. And while writing this book, I did extensive research and interviews and pushed to make the central ideas brief and clear, that is, to write them "on the head of a pin."

Some of what it contains is idealistic, as I believe that life and by extension business should be an ongoing effort to improve and expand. Some of what it says will be obvious one day, but when starting out simple things are often not obvious at all. Some of it is my opinion, with all the shortcomings they contain, and there are ideas that contradict each other because there is no one right way to run a job, hire an employee, or establish and manage a business. I believe the book gets to the heart of the business and addresses much of what will be encountered along the way.

Establishing and growing a construction company can be exasperating, because it is complex and there are few absolute rules, and exhilarating, because the way is open for originality and problem solving. It is a path with great freedom and creativity, and if one persists, there remains a fundamental value in the process and the result.

"Being an optimist is a prerequisite for anybody
who wants to build, because construction
is a matter of optimism; it's a matter of
facing the future with confidence."
—Cesar Pelli

RULES, ETHICS, & OPINIONS

HONESTY: ethical in intention and action.

In building, as in life, decisions are made based on an exchange of information, knowledge, and opinion. If there is reason to mistrust what is said, the process becomes difficult and relationships suspect. Therefore, honesty is a builder's most basic tool and a customer's most basic requirement. Lying is an attempt to avoid the consequences of one's actions and it works out well only in the imagination. Honesty accepts responsibility for those actions and the lessons that accompany them. Simple honesty is the surest way to keep relationships and jobs on track.

> "I believe fundamental honesty is the keystone of business." —Harvey Firestone

INTEGRITY: consistently choosing high morals in one's words and deeds.

Integrity is honesty woven throughout one's life. It is the product of choosing to do the right thing over and over again, even when it appears that it is going to hurt and even when you are the only one who knows.

> "Integrity has no need of rules." —Albert Camus

COMMUNICATION: the exchange of ideas and information.

Good communication informs each party what the other will and will not do, and it helps form strong relationships that can be relied upon. It also addresses the undercurrent of fears, hopes, and demands, which if left unspoken, will disrupt the job with the certainty of tomorrow's sunrise. Further, clear communication tends to discourage the difficult customers and attract the good ones. Like any skill it must be learned and practiced. Begin by listening carefully and speaking clearly. Do not assume anything. Follow every thought and ask every question, including the hard ones. Check often to be sure what was heard is what was meant, by repeating it back for confirmation.

> "The way we communicate with others and with
>   ourselves ultimately determines the quality of our
>   lives." —Anthony Robbins

EDUCATION: knowledge gained through personal effort.

Expertise comes with time and experience, but education will radically accelerate the process. It will improve the long-term success of your building career and the overall quality and organization of your company. It does not necessarily mean college or trade school, but it does mean a lifelong habit of gathering information from all available sources and using it to your benefit.

> "Learning is not attained by chance, it must
>   be sought for with ardor and diligence."
>   —Abigail Adams

QUALITY: great excellence.

Quality, like honesty, is not optional. Nearly everyone knows the difference between a mediocre and a quality product; the best employees want to produce it and the best customers will pay for it. Selling quality instead of price will bring more interesting and more profitable jobs. Make it a cornerstone of your business. Having said that, know that there is a standard for each type of work that is "good enough"; cabinet making is more exacting than trim, and trim requires more care than framing. If cabinet making standards are applied to framing, few people will be able to afford the work.

> "Quality is never an accident; it is always the result of high intention, sincere effort, intelligent direction and skillful execution; it represents the wise choice of many alternatives." —William A. Foster

ATTITUDE: a state of mind or feeling.

Of course customers expect competence, but the most successful people are also liked and respected. Construction is a series of choices, problems, and compromises. Every problem will be solved and every compromise reached without exception, but you choose how to work through that process: by avoiding responsibility, blaming, being defensive and angry, or by taking responsibility and relying on your talents and systems, calmly and professionally. Your cumulative choices determine the atmosphere of the job and the long-term success of the company.[1]

> "The only thing we can do is play on the
> string we have, and that is our attitude. I am
> convinced that life is 10 percent what happens
> to me and 90 percent how I react to it. And so
> it is with you…we are in charge of our attitudes."
> —Charles Swindoll

IMAGE: a mental representation of a thing.

The image of your company, its physical appearance, matters. Customers hire individuals and companies that are clean-cut and well organized because they believe that it indicates competence, quality, and professionalism. And they believe this because, on balance, it does.

---

1   A friend worked for a major U.S. company for his entire career, overseeing construction projects worth tens of millions of dollars, and hiring general contractors to build the projects out. The company required competitive bids on every project from a group of prequalified contractors. But after carefully reviewing the bids, the hiring team did not select primarily on price, but on how the GC and his staff approached and solved problems—that is, if they were calm, level-headed, and took responsibility for their mistakes—and if the hiring team believed that the contractor and his staff would work well with their own staff.

VISION, GOALS: vision is an expression of one's highest aspirations in life. It is a mental image of the way something could be. Goals are the broad but specific outcomes you would accomplish to attain the vision.

From the type of work you pursue, to the employees you hire, to the company systems you develop, every choice defines and furthers your vision and goals. Therefore, keep them in the forefront of your mind by writing them down, reading them often, and revising and updating them regularly.[2] This will cause you to make decisions and follow directions that will produce the results you seek. Keep them simple and flexible; circumstances will change, what is important will change, problems will arise, and opportunities appear. The act of choosing is a tremendously powerful tool and with reasonable, and even somewhat unreasonable goals, if you persist, you will achieve them.

> "So many of our dreams at first seem impossible, then they seem improbable, and then when we summon the will, they soon become inevitable."
> —Christopher Reeve

---

2   *The Seven Habits of Highly Effective People* by Stephen Covey is an excellent book on defining and achieving goals.

PERSISTENCE: to endure tenaciously.

Sometimes the only distinction between success and failure is the next attempt at making a thing work. Achieving a goal, business or personal, is dependent on being clear about what you want, working hard to achieve it, making changes as required, continuing to expand your knowledge, and sticking with what you are doing until it works. [3]

> "For me, many long evenings of study led to precise rules, disciplines, and a plan that finally worked. Luck had nothing to do with it; it was persistence and hard work." —William O'Neil

SAFETY: freedom from injury or risk.

The pain of a person hurt is obvious, less obvious are the ways a company suffers; job disruption, lost income, rising insurance costs, poor morale, schedule changes, and possible legal issues. A safe job is the direct result of the effort and resources that a company gives to safety, and the investment pays for itself a thousandfold, although the return is measured by what does not happen.

---

3   This idea, although true, does not go quite far enough. Again and again in business literature you will read about the importance of persistence—Edison's 10,000 tries to create a light bulb is a favorite—but nothing will make a bad idea work and there is no value in obstinately climbing the wrong mountain.

PACING: steady persistent effort toward a goal.

Many new builders act as if ever-increasing intensity and limitless hard work assure success. But building is by nature fast-paced, hard work, and no one can maintain a frantic pace over long periods of time and succeed. Don't confuse the natural intensity of the industry with a management style that is always in crisis and that will consume every ounce of energy you have and still require more.

> "If we agree that the bottom line of life is happiness, not success, then it makes perfect sense to say that it is the journey that counts, not reaching the destination." —Mihaly Csikszentmihalyi

———————

FEAR: anticipation of danger or pain. Dread, concern, regret, fright, worry.

There are two types of fear: our natural reaction to physical danger—which is instinctual and at least partly beyond our control—and the psychological stuff our mind makes up. Everyone experiences both types, it is part of the human condition, but those who succeed look squarely at their fear and do what is required anyway.

> "I learned that courage was not the absence of fear, but the triumph over it. The brave man is not he who does not feel afraid, but he who conquers that fear." —Nelson Mandela

———————

MARKETING & SALES: marketing is the process of attracting prospective buyers, sales is influencing them to buy your product.

Sales begin with marketing and marketing begins with providing a service good enough that a high percentage of customers arrive wanting to buy from you. Many builders choose to see themselves as craftsmen while viewing marketing and sales as necessary evils requiring little attention or believing they will take care of themselves; they aren't and they won't. Create an exceptional marketing and sales organization.

"Keep in mind selling isn't manipulating, pressuring, or cajoling. Selling is explaining the logic and benefits of a decision or position. Selling is convincing other people to work with you. Selling is overcoming objections and roadblocks." —Jeff Haden

"The aim of marketing is to know and understand the customer so well the product or service fits him and sells itself."
—Peter Drucker

MONEY: a way to measure value.

For every builder who has made and kept a fortune, there are a hundred who made one and lost it, some several times. When business is good, decisions are made as if the money will continue forever, but construction is a business of cycles, and when work slows a company's weakness shows quickly as its financial obligations overwhelm it. *Learn to manage money.* Take classes, read books, set long-term goals, study business cycles, and understand what it means to overextend. In good times and bad be conservative—even frugal—control spending, keep overhead low, keep loans to a minimum, establish and fund a *cash reserve account*,[4] and build assets.

> "Some of life's greatest enjoyments and many of life's greatest disappointments stem from your decisions about money. Whether you experience great peace of mind or constant anxiety will depend on getting your finances under control."
> —Robert Allen

OVERHEAD is the cost of doing business.

It is the cost of trucks and fuel, phones and computers, stationery and office salaries; it is every expense not tied directly to the cost of construction. Determine what percentage you must add to your estimates to cover overhead and add it to every job from the day you open for business.[5]

---

4   See the Money section for an explanation of a cash reserve account.
5   See Overhead and Profit under Money Definitions for more details.

PROFIT is the reward for running a business well.

There is nothing more fundamental in business than profit. Before you do anything else, learn what it is and how to charge for it and add it to every project. If a business is not making adequate profit, the owner is working for wages and would be better off taking a job with someone else and giving up the responsibility and the risk of being in business.

> "To fail to provide for profit is to subvert all business logic, and to leave you, your employees, and your suppliers at risk." —Bob Hanbury

MANAGEMENT AND ADMINISTRATION, business skills.

Many tradesmen have a fantasy of being so skilled at their craft that great projects and endless work will flow to them while management and administration will take care of themselves; they could not be more wrong. When opening a small construction business, management skills are as important as trade skills, and they quickly become more important as the company grows. If your goal is to be a tradesman work for someone else. If your goal is to establish and build a significant company, put your tool belt aside and focus on business as soon as it is practical.

GRATITUDE: thankfulness, appreciation.

When you feel intense engagement—when love and joy meet in your life—that is gratitude. Appreciation and gratitude are appropriate responses to the wonders of life: light, air, tools, books, family, friends, and a million other things that surround and sustain you. Focus on them and express your appreciation for them often.

> "Gratitude helps you to grow and expand; gratitude brings joy and laughter into your life and into the lives of those around you." —Eileen Caddy

———————

HUMILITY: The quality of being modest and respectful.

Ego—me mine I—divides, attempting to make oneself special and others less than, and it inflates itself and therefore must attack others to defend its positions, usually angrily, and always to its own detriment. A huge ego is a sign of intense fear. And that fear is expressed as arrogance or bullying and it damages relationships and itself. The modest have no reason to inflate themselves and thus little to fear and nothing to defend. They can be creative, confident, motivational and make hard calls, but they are often quiet, listening, asking questions, encouraging, and facilitating others' ideas and efforts. Humility joins with others to make the best of each situation, and it allows one to learn from everyone: the housewife, the business titan, and the ditch digger.

> "Humility is the surest sign of strength."
> —Thomas Merton

———————

BUILDER

Builder,[6] one whose occupation is that of pricing, organizing, and building; one who controls or directs the work of construction.

Contractor, one who signs a contract and assumes responsibility to install, construct, rebuild, organize, or manage the building of something.

General Contractor (GC), a company that has the primary contract on a project and is charged with getting the work done as detailed on the plans and specifications. The GC represents the clients and it is the GC's responsibility to be certain the clients get what they are paying for from subs, suppliers, and employees. GCs usually run several projects simultaneously.

Project Manager (PM), Superintendent, Foreman, is the individual in a company primarily responsible for directing a single project from beginning to end. The name used depends on a company's size and organizational structure.

Construction Management (CM), in residential work this is a term generally reserved for companies that act as

6   Throughout this book I have used the term *builder* primarily to indicate a general contractor (GC) and occasionally to refer to a tradesman or subcontractor.

the client's representative and manage the construction process but have no field employees.[7]

Owners' Representative, a person or a firm representing the clients' interests in the construction process.

Stand on any street in any town and look around. Everything that you see, everything behind the walls, under the street, and over your head was put into place by a builder. Building is a science requiring organization and engineering and an art requiring creativity and communication. If you include all types of construction—residential, commercial, industrial, dams, highways, tunnels, airports, pipelines—it is an enormous industry.

This book is concerned with residential construction, including the maintenance, restoration, renovation, and construction of private homes and related properties; it is written for the guy installing a door handle and the company building several homes.[8] The industry is divided into the following general categories, each with a great deal of overlap:

1. Restoration—bringing all or part of a historically significant property back to its original condition.

2. Remodeling-additions—renovating all or part of or adding onto an existing home.

3. New homes

    a. Custom home, one-offs for a client on his lot or yours.

---

7   By definition, a good GC manages projects and represents the client, therefore the distinction between a CM and a GC in residential work, except perhaps on extremely high-end projects, is minimal.

8   Companies building huge track developments and apartment complexes are commercial builders, although the cutoff point between a large residential builder and a commercial builder is not clearly defined.

  b. Building homes on speculation,[9] one or several at a time.

  c. Developing land—subdividing the property, installing streets and utilities—to sell lots and homes to clients or to sell just the lots to clients or other builders.

4. The unusual—log homes, straw bale, tree houses, tiny homes, panelized, block, or rammed earth construction.[10] There are many wonderful and useful nonstandard construction methods available.

5. The specialty—fire restoration, flood damage. These are typically connected to work for or through an insurance company to cover its policyholder's claim.

The individuals and companies that do residential work may be divided roughly into the following categories:

1. Handyman services, small repairs and improvements to existing grounds, structures, and systems.

2. Trades,[11] there are dozens of trades and many of these have subcategories, a flooring company installing only wood flooring or a concrete company specializing in concrete patios, for example. Trades appear and disappear as methods and materials change, and individuals move from being generalists to specialists and back again as the economy

9 Speculative home building involves a company buying land and building homes in advance of having them sold, gambling that there will be demand for the finished product. Spec homes may be built with zero client input, that is, all of the details and finishes are chosen by the builder; or with some input from the buyer, paint colors and floor finishes, for example; or with nearly everything being chosen by the client, effectively making it a custom home.

10 In Wikipedia see "building material" for a brief overview of various building materials and how they are used.

11 The terms *trade* or *tradesman* refer to any skilled person providing a specific type of construction: mason, plumber, or someone hanging wallpaper, for example.

fluctuates. When a trade company does work for a homeowner, it is a business providing a service; when it works for a general contractor, it is a subcontractor.

3. Specialty firms, design and build a certain type of project, such as steel buildings, kitchens, or sunrooms, for example. These firms are not considered a trade because there are multiple layers to their service, and they are not generally considered a GC because what they do is confined to a specific type of work.

4. General Contractor (GC),[12]

    a. A small general contractor has a yearly gross income from zero to $500,000. The owner almost always works in the field, often doing estimating-sales-administrative tasks evenings and weekends. Depending on the type of business, this company will often work on one or two jobs. Payroll and taxes are likely to be handled by an outside vendor. There will be one to five field employees and various subcontractors. The company office is likely to be in the home and it may or may not have a shop. It will own many hand tools and a few vehicles but no large construction equipment.

    b. A midsize GC, yearly income up to $2 million. The owner will rarely work in the field, instead being responsible for overseeing jobs, estimating-sales, and overall management. There will be five to twenty or so field employees with a large number of subs. There will be, depending on the dollar value of each, from one to ten jobs

---

12 The dollar figures and organizational descriptions are a *rough approximation* and are provided to give a general sense of size and organization.

running with several in the sales pipeline. There
may be a general manager and some supervisory
field employees. There will be an estimator-sales
staff, a full-time accountant-bookkeeper, and
at least one full-time office administrator. They
will have office space—if it remains in the home
the area will be dedicated to the business—often
with a shop, several vehicles, a great deal of
small tools and equipment, and depending
on the type of work performed, some large
construction equipment. A formal management
hierarchy will be in place or forming

c. A large residential GC, yearly income from
$2 million to $5 million.[13] The owner is a
full-time business manager overseeing several
departments and the company's overall form,
growth, and direction. The company will be
running from five to twenty jobs, depending
on their dollar values, with many in the
sales pipeline. The office will include several
full-time estimating-sales and design-drafting
staff members, an accounting department, an
office manager with administrative help. There
will be a formal management structure. There
may be engineers or designers on staff. For
those companies with trades working in the
field (as opposed to those that sub everything)
there will be a shop, an equipment mechanic,
and a great deal of construction equipment.

The stages described for a GC will roughly correspond
to the stages that residential construction companies pass
through as they are established and grow. A company grows

13 There are commercial and industrial general contractors with yearly
volume in the tens of millions of dollars.

as the knowledge and sophistication of the owner and the organization increase. But know that size is no indication of success. Many large companies are a rat's nest of poor organization and unhappy people while many small and midsized companies provide an excellent living and sense of community for employees and owners.

"Nothing in the world can take the place of persistence. Talent will not; nothing is more common than unsuccessful men with talent. Genius will not; unrewarded genius is almost a proverb. Education will not; the world is full of educated derelicts. Persistence and determination alone are omnipotent."
—Calvin Coolidge

BUILDER NOTES

Principles

A successful GC, the short version: quality product, great employees, great clients, solid financial controls, accurate estimates, and a constant effort to learn, grow, and improve.

> It takes 20 years to build a reputation and five minutes to ruin it. If you think about that, you'll do things differently." —Warren Buffett

---

Seeing a problem and choosing to ignore it is always a bad idea.

> "Most people spend more time and energy going around problems than in trying to solve them."
> —Henry Ford

Your business is not you. It is an entity, existing apart from you, having needs—capital, profit, organization, and attention—and its money is not yours. It belongs to suppliers, subs, employees, and taxes. If there is a consistent profit and a decision is made to pay some of that profit out, only then does it become your money.

Be honest, even when it hurts; but not when it is an opinion, which will pointlessly confuse, hurt, or offend another.

> "Laughing at our mistakes can lengthen our own life. Laughing at someone else's can shorten it."
> —Cullen Hightower

Don't let success ruin you. Time and again when builders feel they are on top of the world, they stop doing the basics: treating others with respect, managing money conservatively, and focusing on the core of their business. Relax. Remain modest and grateful. Continue to do what got you here in the first place. Regardless of the degree of prosperity you enjoy, maintain a healthy sense of humor and realize that in good times and bad, everything changes.

> "Success is a lousy teacher. It seduces smart people
> into thinking they can't lose." —Bill Gates

Break every large task, goal, or project into smaller parts. Challenges that seem overwhelming become manageable as a series of smaller tasks. Do the first task, the second, the third, and so on, until the job is complete.

> "Energy & persistence conquer all things."
> —Benjamin Franklin

Being exceptional at what you do offers several advantages; the highly skilled tend to get the best jobs. Because the clients are satisfied, there are fewer problems; they are more likely to stay busy during industry slowdowns; generally they get paid more; and it is immensely satisfying to produce an excellent product.

There is no such thing as a perfect job or a perfectly satisfied customer. The world is not a perfect place. Therefore, strive to provide excellent quality and service—to exceed expectations—while leaving perfection to others.

> "Striving for excellence motivates you; striving for
> perfection is demoralizing." —Harriet Braiker

Learn to distinguish between that which is done well and that which is not. Imitate and improve on the best of what you find.

Business Strategies

A basic structure underlies every company. A consciously developed structure is more effective than one that develops organically. Study how the most successful companies are organized and imitate them.[14]

Do not slow or stop marketing in anticipation of winning a job. Projects fall through for a thousand reasons and often at the last minute. If marketing has been slowed or abandoned, the damage from the loss of that job will be even worse. Further, if you become entirely dependent on a specific job, you may agree to unfavorable contract terms because you can't afford to lose the work. If marketing brings in too much work, tighten your qualifications or explain that you cannot take on more work at that time. This is a much better problem to have then struggling to find work at the last minute.

> "Be persistent and work hard: success is a marathon, not a sprint. Never give up." —Anonymous

---

Look at both sides of new business ideas. Give as much weight to what could go wrong as to what could go right. Enthusiasm and imagination often make ideas appear far better than they really are. Research the idea. Map it out. Make a list of what-ifs. Talk with others. Give it time to simmer—a few weeks or months—and see if it stands up to reexamination.

---

14 Read "Service Through Structure," in *The Journal of Light Construction (JLC)* archives.

If you love what you do, the money will follow. No, it won't. If you work hard, find and keep great employees, provide an excellent product, charge enough, control spending, save money, and market to the right customers, it might. In a moment of exuberance people explain their success as resulting from loving what they do, but each of them touched just the right stones to cross the brook.

Failure, although usually painful, is a compelling teacher and if the lesson is learned, it provides guidance for the next attempt.

> "Failure is simply the opportunity to begin again,
> this time more intelligently." —Henry Ford

A basic business plan is important when starting out.[15] Address the fundamental questions: Is there a market? What skills and resources are required? How will I get customers? What area will I work in? Who is the competition? What is my budget? Do I have enough capital? In the process of asking and answering questions you will create a clear road map for the first few years of the business.[16]

Be patient and selective when looking for work. There is no point in getting a job without profit or with a bad customer.

It's hard to be successful if you live in a depressed area of the country. You may need to move to a more prosperous area in order to run a successful construction company.

---

15 There are large formal business plans—containing perhaps fifty to a hundred pages with dozens of graphs, charts, and projections. These are the ones usually recommended in books and by people trying to be helpful, but they are far too complex and expensive for a small business.

16 The Small Business Administration (SBA) and SCORE Association have business plan forms available for free on their websites, and there are other sources on the web.

Do not pursue jobs you do not have the skill and resources to do well. It can be tempting to try for everything that comes your way, but you are likely to fail if your grasp exceeds your ability by too much. Be patient. Do the work you know well and expand thoughtfully as your knowledge and the company's capacity increases.

———————

It is possible to start planning and gathering quotes for a job too early. If you begin too soon many of the details and the reasons for decisions will be forgotten while suppliers and subcontractor quotes will expire. Further, the job may be cancelled or change significantly. Try to begin job preparation so you can move smoothly from planning into building with little or no time delay.

———————

Avoid make-work projects during slow work periods. As critical as good employees are, making up work to keep people employed drains cash and may cause long-term financial damage to the company. If you have run out of work, your marketing is inadequate or there is an economic slowdown. In either case recovery is going to take time and chances are it is better to lay people off to conserve cash and allow the business to survive.

———————

Do not inflate prices to turn away work. You want even the people you don't work for to think well of your company, and a wildly high price will offend. Better ways to slow growth include reducing advertising, being more selective in the jobs you look at, and telling clients honestly—including a margin for error—how long it will be until you will be ready to do their work.

———————

Don't procrastinate. Putting off a decision because of fear or uncertainty is worse than being wrong. In business, hundreds of decisions must be made; many are obvious, some require discussion, while others require gathering information, reflection, and consulting with professionals. Some decisions will be inspired, most will get the job done, and some will be wrong. Make the best decisions you can, learn from your mistakes, and move on.

> "I've missed more than 9000 shots in my career.
> I've lost almost 300 games. 26 times, I've been
> trusted to take the game winning shot and missed.
> I've failed over and over and over again in my life.
> And that is why I succeed." —Michael Jordan

———

Construction is a business of cycles—based on reputation, the economy, and the region of the country—and while it is true that better managers will level out the peaks and valleys somewhat, the best and the worst go through cycles of feast and famine.

———

Develop a clear and sustainable marketing plan and maintain it over the long term. Implementing a marketing plan that starts with a bang and quickly peters-out is a waste of time and money. If marketing is not your strong suit think about hiring someone to do it for you.

———

Too much work will kill a company just as surely as not enough. Over time too much work will overwhelm the people and systems, service and product will suffer, customers will be dissatisfied, and staff will become disgruntled.

———

Do not leave a job before it is done to work on another one. This is a common practice among badly run companies, and it is caused by poor cash flow—that is, starting another job to get cash from the first draw because you don't have enough money to pay bills—or poor planning. In either case, the company is in trouble. There are times when leaving a job is okay—bad weather, material delays, not being paid—but as an exception, not as a normal way of operating. It costs a great deal of money to move on and off jobs, and it will quickly cost the customer's good will. Develop a system for scheduling jobs, charge enough, manage money tightly, and complete each job before moving to the next one.

> "We are what we repeatedly do. Excellence, then,
> is not an act but a habit." —Aristotle

Encourage creative differences of opinion. Constructive conflict can result in better ideas and procedures, and, over time, stronger relationships. If disagreements are handled directly (not avoided) and worked through fairly, the result will often provide the best possible solution to a problem. Such communication requires honest intentions and emotional maturity, that is: controlling anger; not trying to "win" or best the other; not making ridiculous claims, absurd demands, or dictatorial decisions; not blaming or attacking; and not giving up.

> "Conflict is inevitable, but combat is optional."
> —Max Lucado

Be wary of new products that have not had time to prove themselves in the field. New products can offer important advances, but there have been hundreds of products from new and established companies that have appeared and disappeared, some leaving a trail of lawsuits and angry customers in their wake. Even if a product from a new company does not fail, you run the risk of the company going out of business and having no one to replace parts or cover warranties. It is generally best to use well-established products and let others experiment with the new stuff.

Be reluctant to add the cost of large construction equipment to overhead. Many builders buy equipment—a bobcat or a dump truck, for example—because they feel they are paying too much to a subcontractor or to rent one, or because they feel they can afford it and the idea of owning it excites them. But construction equipment is a depreciating asset, that is, the value of it decreases with use and age, and as the item is used, repair costs rise. Further, in six months you may not need it but the payments, insurance, depreciation, maintenance, and storage costs will continue. Unless there is an irrefutable and long-term need for equipment, use a subcontractor or rent what you need.

Do not underpay yourself. Business owners sometimes pay themselves a low salary believing that keeping cash in the business will help it to grow. When starting out there may be a period where you don't take much out, but once the company is up and running, you and everyone involved should be getting a fair wage. Not paying full salaries could hide the fact that you are not making enough money to justify being in business.

Pay your taxes. Young companies sometimes put off paying taxes because they are short on cash and figure that they will catch up later. This is a mistake on the same scale as the captain of the *Titanic* believing that no iceberg could sink his ship. Taxes are not optional and they cannot be put off until you have free cash. Set money aside in a separate account and pay your taxes fully and on time.

___

Practices, Off the Job and On

Get the required business licenses. In many areas of the country, state and local authorities require licenses. Although people do operate without proper licensing, they always have a nagging sense that they will be caught and this will permeate their personal and professional lives. Further, when there is a problem, they will not be covered by insurance, and in some states they sacrifice protection from the court systems,[17] and open themselves to lawsuits and, in extreme cases, jail. As complex and seemingly pointless as the licensing process sometimes appears to be, ultimately it benefits everyone by leveling the playing field and increasing professionalism.

___

Start with simple procedures and systems. Procedures are the steps required to track and record information. Systems are the processes that record, measure, and compare the statistics of a company, an accounting program, for example. If you begin with procedures and systems that are too complex they will use significant resources and provide mountains of useless information—or fall out of use completely.

___

17 In California, and perhaps in other states, unlicensed contractors or subcontractors—even if they don't have a license for only a portion of the job—cannot sue their client. That is, if a client does not pay their bill, those without a license cannot take them to court to recover the loss because the courts will not hear the case.

Write the date and time on everything that you work with: plans, letters, notes, sections in books, when someone said something, when you bought new equipment, and when something is supposed to happen. Do it so much that it becomes second nature.

Keep inventory to a minimum. Inventory—lumber, hardware, and paint, for example—ties up cash and space, and the material must be handled repeatedly as it is bought, stored, moved around, and brought to the job. In certain trades you may need inventory, but keep it to a minimum, track it carefully (use an inventory system), and protect it from weather, theft, and damage. Unless you have a clear need to hold inventory, buy the bulk of what is required on an as-needed basis.

Keep an orderly job site. An organized job site offers important benefits: it is safer, the customer appreciates it, work moves faster because people are not working around trash and they can find what they are looking for, materials get damaged or lost less, installed work is damaged less, problems are easier to see, and it is a more enjoyable place to work.

Cutting corners to save money or time will cost more of both. Some examples: working off ladders instead of setting up scaffolding, digging a trench without shoring, setting trusses by hand when a crane is required. It may seem to work, but the cost will be paid in some other way: by sacrificing safety or quality or by demanding too much of workmen. Obviously it is important to do each job as quickly and economically as possible, but time and financial pressure cannot be allowed to create hazardous or needlessly difficult conditions.

> "A little neglect may breed great mischief."
> —Benjamin Franklin

Listen closely when a client is upset about a problem. Don't be defensive or make excuses. If possible, correct the problem immediately. Otherwise, make a plan and a time line, keep the client informed, and make the correction as soon as possible.

Develop flexible systems for the field. The most inconceivable things stop or delay jobs: high wind, low water pressure, a stripped screw, a broken tool. Therefore, develop systems that facilitate fast solutions and empower employees to solve problems: have a well-stocked truck or trailer with tools and miscellaneous supplies, reference books handy, a designated runner who knows the area and the suppliers, and have a list of other work that may be performed while a solution is found.

Regularly schedule safety meetings. Make attendance mandatory and don't allow them to be taken lightly. Replace people who won't cooperate. Set up a serious safety program to educate new and current employees on safe work habits. Make a safe job site one of the foreman's key responsibilities and insist on commonsense safety from employees and subs. Buy the best tools and equipment available and immediately replace or repair unsafe items. Have a first aid kit available on every job and be sure folks know how to use it. Encourage people to take a first aid class; you take one first.[18]

---

18 The American Red Cross provides first aid classes at various sites around the United States. Also, search for articles in *The Journal of Light Construction* on job safety, for example, "Managing Job Site Safety," from the January 1989 issue.

Document unresolved job disputes. When there is a dispute on a job but work can't be stopped to resolve it, write a letter to the participants documenting the details and the issues and explain that the parties have agreed to resolve them at a later date. Let them know the letter is coming (don't spring it on them) and state only facts without blame or recrimination. When there is time to resolve the issue, this document will provide details about what happened and help to shape the conversation.

Early in my career, I saved pieces of plywood, scraps of lumber, open paint cans and caulk, odd fixtures and hardware, but found that by the time I got around to using it, most of it was damaged or moving, storing, and working around it had cost far more than buying it new would have. Most of the random material leftover at the end of a job is better given to a tradesman or the client—or thrown away.

As each job ends review what worked and what did not. Document both and use these lessons to improve the company and the next job.

> "There is no secret to success. It is the result of preparation, hard work, and learning from failure."
> —Colin Powell

Human Relations

Offer ongoing education to employees. Share relevant articles, have company classes on important issues, ask people inside the company to teach what they know best, invite folks from outside—suppliers, subs, retired builders—to teach their specialty, buy trade magazine subscriptions for key employees, and send your best people to seminars and trade shows when you can afford it.[19]

> "The only sure weapon against bad ideas is
> better ideas. The source of better ideas is
> wisdom. The surest path to wisdom is education."
> —Alfred Griswold

When hiring members of the same family or close friends, their loyalty may be to each other not the company. If there are problems with one they may react as a group, and you will have two or three angry employees instead of one. They also may cover for each other or all quit at once.[20]

Do not hire illegal workers. It lowers your community's standard of living by lowering wages. It breaks the law. It puts your insurance coverage at risk. And it often lowers the quality of the finished product. Insist on seeing documentation for everyone about whom there is a question.[21]

---

19 There are good and bad seminars; research those you are interested in to be certain there is substance to them.

20 We had a foreman who allowed his boyhood friend, a guy we hired on the foreman's recommendation, to sleep on the job when he had been out partying the night before, which apparently he did often.

21 I love Immigration and know that it is part of what makes this country amazing. But the U.S. government has been criminally negligent in not enforcing its own immigration laws, allowing them to be reduced to personal opinion, and, in the process, mocking the effort of those who do what is required to be here legally.

Keep the same crew on a job from start to finish. Each time a new crew arrives on a job they begin from scratch; this costs time, money, and the client's good will. On the other hand, a crew that returns to the same job every day knows what needs to be done, they know how to work on the site, and they have relationships with everyone involved. Further, the same crew—having built the job from start to finish—will take pride in the project.[22]

Treat laborers well. A laborer is anyone who works at the unskilled portion of construction: a carpenter's helper, a ditch digger, or the guy moving material and cleaning the job site. Sometimes a laborer works as an apprentice, either officially as in a union or informally with a non-union company. Laborers tend to be younger although some laborers do it as a career. A good laborer is a significant asset. Encourage them to learn, don't overwork them, and vary what they do in order to keep them interested.

Do not allow any one person to become indispensable or to have knowledge or skills unknown to others in the organization. If they leave the damage can be extensive and in some cases irreversible.

Spend a large percentage of your marketing budget keeping your name in front of past clients. That is where your best leads come from.

---

22 Look into the "Lead Carpenter System" as a method of organizing the field. See HomeTech Publishing's website, The National Association of Home Builders' *The Lead Carpenter System: A Guide for Remodelers,* and trade magazines for details. In my experience, there are situations in which the "Lead Carpenter System" works, but there are also times and types of work when it does not.

Be calmly persistent. It is easier and more effective to call and re-call someone who is not doing what they need to do rather than calling once and getting angry. Depending on how soon you need something, call every week, day, or hour—being firm but calm, even friendly—reminding them that something is supposed to happen. Some folks will be annoyed, but if they are not doing what they have agreed to do, let that be their problem. Develop a method of tracking whom you called, what was said, when they are supposed to act, and when to call them back.[23] Of course, if you have to remind someone to do his job often, it is time to find someone else.

Work with people who share your values. The attitudes and actions of those around you directly affect the quality of your life and the success of your business. Therefore, work with and around people who model honesty, hard work, optimism, and a generous spirit. Avoid those who don't.

"Pick out associates whose behavior is better than yours and you'll drift in that direction." —Warren Buffett

---

Learn from subs. Ask a really good electrician about the ways power enters a building, how it is measured and dispersed. Ask about junction boxes and breakers and subpanels, and what options exist for wiring, lights, switches, and backup systems. Ask what distinguishes an excellent job from a poor one and where a bad sub cuts corners. Over time, ask the best of every trade the same types of questions and learn to distinguish really good work from poor work. And consider taking a beginner's class in a couple of trades that interest you to gain a broader understanding of the industry.

---

23 Microsoft Outlook works well for this purpose.

Anger makes us stupid, as individuals and as a group. Expressing intense anger—besides alienating those around you and causing more problems—makes it impossible to see solutions. You will feel anger and frustration, of course, but maturity and professionalism is about channeling strong emotions along constructive paths. [24]

> "Anger, if not restrained, is frequently more
> hurtful to us than the injury that provoked it."
> —Lucius Seneca

———

Underpromise and overdeliver. If you make grand promises about your abilities and fall short, the client will remember. If, on the other hand, you sell solid performance but deliver exceptional results, most clients will recommend you to anyone who will listen.

———

Referrals are your best source of work. Referrals from past clients, subs, suppliers, designers, friends, and family provide the best chance of getting the work, of the job going well, and of forming lasting relationships.

———

Loyalty is crucial, but don't let it blind you to what needs to be done. There will be times when you need to stop using a sub or a supplier or fire an employee. Don't avoid these decisions by hoping things will improve or pretending they are not as bad as they are. Make the difficult decisions and move on.

———

24 If you have a problem with anger—that is, if it bursts forth seemingly beyond your control—get help from a wise friend or therapist and consider reading books like Gerald G. Jampolsky's "Love Is Letting Go Of Fear". Although it may not seem like it, anger comes from fear, not what someone else did or did not do, and it is always within our control.

Your company is more than its trade. Despite what you may think, your company is not in the business of installing plumbing or insulating a house; it is in the business of understanding what the customer wants within the scope of your trade and giving it to them in the most professional manner possible.

———————

Be concerned if a potential client is distracted or hard to reach. If you are invited to bid on a project, the client should be accessible—take or return calls and be willing to answer whatever questions arise—and if they aren't they are almost certainly fishing for prices, not actually going to do the work, or they already know who they are going to use.

———————

See excellent builders as motivation and inspiration, not competition.

———————

Join a group of builders who meet to discuss shared issues and ideas. This connection can help to establish new relationships and to provide business opportunities. There are business-networking organizations—meetup.com for example—that facilitate such groups. If you don't find a group in your area, start one. A dynamic peer group is a powerful learning and motivational tool.

> "Many of us are direct competitors, but we have more to gain by banding together and raising local standards than we do by working in isolation."
> —Dan Kolbert

———————

When asked to bid with builders or design firms, know that they are looking for someone to help solve problems, not create them with caveats, exceptions, or attitude. No one is interested in working with a prima donna or with someone who acts as if they are doing them a favor. Be friendly and professional and get back to them quickly with the information requested. If you are not interested, say so immediately and don't waste their time.

> "The most important single ingredient in the formula of success is knowing how to get along with people." —Theodore Roosevelt

---

Thank people who refer clients to you with a thank-you card or perhaps a small gift. Give the same thing to everyone. Never get involved in owing people favors or paybacks for references.

Don't begrudge others a fair profit. You plan on making a profit and others must too. Besides, prosperity is contagious.

Although partnerships can work, in construction, most don't. If you are considering a partnership, choose your partner with great care. Skills and assets are important; temperament and character are more important. Do not make a decision based on the excitement of the moment. Review a potential partner's work history. Detail his strengths and weaknesses. List the benefits he brings to the partnership. Discuss each other's ideas and expectations at length and ask lots of hard questions. If you decide to go ahead, write out what you have agreed to, both to understand each other's point of view and for legal reasons. Consider involving a lawyer in the writing of the partnership agreement and include a plan of dissolution in case there are irreconcilable differences.

Talk about business issues with the appropriate people. Bragging about success, lamenting problems, or speaking badly of others will come back to hurt you in unexpected and sometimes devastating ways.

> "Speak ill of no man, but speak all the good you know of everybody." —Benjamin Franklin

———————

Get it in writing. Although it is easier to trust others—to work on a handshake—the reality of business is that the more your company relies on contracts the more likely it is to succeed for the long term.

———————

Being A Builder

Ask questions and seek advice from the wisest people you can find. Have you heard this one? "When I was a boy of fourteen, my father was so ignorant I could hardly stand to have the old man around. But when I got to be twenty-one, I was astonished at how much the old man had learned in seven years."[25] While youth brings energy and enthusiasm it also brings impatience—and often arrogance—as well as limited knowledge and experience. Therefore, seek advice from the wisest people you can find and listen closely to their answers.

> "It ain't what you don't know that gets you into trouble. It's what you know for sure that just ain't so." —Mark Twain

———————

25 Mark Twain

Never stop learning, expanding, and growing. Go to seminars, take courses, stop at building projects. Look around, take photos, ask questions. Read books and trade journals (begin a library of the most useful ones), search the web, spend time at suppliers looking at the inventory and asking questions. Take home and study product cut sheets and catalogs, talk with tradesmen and business owners, visit trade shows, get to know other builders, join a building association and take full advantage of what they offer.[26]

> "All true education is self-education." —Lee Johnson

Pay attention to current and historic business cycles. The overall national economy affects your business directly. HUD's U.S. Housing Market Conditions Report and the Case/Shiller Index are economic indicators of the construction activity in the United States. Familiarize yourself with these and other indicators and watch them to understand the larger market of which your business is a part.

Give time to all major decisions. It is the way the human brain works best: gather information, process it, develop questions, get answers, process them, ask more questions—and then take action. Give yourself time to follow this process with all major decisions.

> "You're neither right nor wrong because people agree with you. You're right because your facts and your reasoning are right." —Warren Buffett

---

26 SCORE is a nonprofit volunteer organization of retired business people that bills itself as "Counselors to America's Small Business" with free and confidential advice available. www.score.org.

You cannot do everything. No one can be a tradesman in the morning, a bookkeeper in the afternoon, and a designer in the evening and be really good at any of them. "Jack of all trades, master of none" captures the essence of this idea, and the phrase refers to a person whose knowledge and skill, while broad, is superficial. Choose a few things to be exceptional at and hire the best employees, subs, and professionals you can find to excel in other areas.

> "Those who are jacks-of-all-trades and masters of
> none are rarely dramatically successful in any field."
> —William O'Neil

It is more useful to know where to get information than it is to try to remember everything. This is true first because you cannot remember all that you need to know and second because varying methods, designs, and products have been developed and conflicting and sometimes wrong information is circulated. Regularly researching products and methods will increase your knowledge and keep your techniques current.

Scan the local newspaper daily. You will learn things that might affect your business; for example which building permits were issued or who declared bankruptcy. And consider scanning the business section of a national newspaper like *Investor's Business Daily* (IBD) or *The Wall Street Journal* (WSJ) once a week to learn about and keep up with broad economic issues.

Being connected to the building process by coming up through the trades will teach you things that coming at it in any other way cannot.

Avoid the idea that because you have been a builder for a number of years you know all there is to know. This subtle arrogance will keep you from gaining new knowledge. Never stop seeking new ideas and information.

> "Something in human nature causes us to
> start slacking off at our moment of greatest
> accomplishment. As you become successful, you
> will need a great deal of self discipline not to lose
> your sense of balance, humility, and commitment."
> —H. Ross Perot

If you get into financial trouble, if your company is barely hanging on, there are examples in trade magazines of people who were in the same situation and either pulled themselves out of it or chose to go under. Read what they have to say.

What you have and what you do is based on those who taught and sustained you and on what others created and built. The idea of the "self-made man" is nonsense. In fact, the wise stand gratefully on the efforts, ideas, and accomplishments of those around them and those who went before.

> "Someone is sitting in the shade today because
> someone planted a tree a long time ago."
> —Warren Buffett

Read trade publications. This is an effective way to find ideas and acquire the skills needed to grow your business. Subscribe to as many good publications as you can read in a month. Save relevant articles and refer to them often. Take the best ideas and implement them in a gradual but continuous process of improvement.[27]

———————

"Argue for your limitations, and
sure enough they're yours."
—Richard Bach

[27] *Fine Home Building, The Journal of Light Construction,* and *Builder* are must-reads. The *Remodeling* website has some good articles. *Consumer Reports* offers reviews and ratings on various construction products and tools. *HomeTechPublishing.com* has a few important articles every builder should read.

PARTICIPANTS

PERSONNEL

People employed in an organization or business.

Employees, workers, staff, workforce.

Personnel department is responsible for keeping records on employees.

The best people—skilled, engaged, committed, reliable, honest—create the best companies, and the best companies—marked by vision, team work, communication, organization, good compensation—attract and keep the best people.

When hiring, choose a positive outlook and innate intelligence first because skills can be taught but character and intelligence provide the most long-term benefit. Integrate each new hire into the organization with an introduction to the company's vision, goals, and structure and reinforce them often through meetings, newsletters, and bulletins, and by creating a strong positive culture. Choose the best people, define their role, allow reasonable autonomy, build in accountability, and share success; most people will thrive in such an environment.

PERSONNEL NOTES

Miscellaneous

Identify your strengths and weaknesses. Take on those things you are best at while delegating those things you don't do well.

_____

Create a company handbook.[28] Keep the first one simple; expand and refine it over time. A handbook should explain what is expected from employees and the things that affect them, such as profit sharing, payday, wages, employment trial periods, holiday and vacation procedures, how criminal records are handled, background checks, which tools the company supplies and which the craftsman provides, when, how, and for what employees are disciplined, and on-the-job standards of personal behavior.[29] Spell out the things that are cause for immediate dismissal—drugs, drinking at work, theft, violence, or harassment. Review the document with all new employees and have them initial each page and sign the entire document. Place the signed copy in their file and give them one for reference. Keep the handbook active by referring to it often and revising it as needed. Each time it is changed pass out the changed section and have employees sign to indicate that they have read and understand the changes. Put an initialed copy in their file. Make the document inclusive but concise; a handbook that is too long, unreadable, or complex will be ignored. The document has legal ramifications so have it reviewed by your attorney.

_____

28 You will find examples of employee manuals in trade magazines or online, and some companies sell them.

29 Establishing rules—such as no swearing, not sharing political opinions, maintaining clean and organized job sites, being friendly and professional, dressing appropriately, no smoking in the home and policing butts outside, for example—is a key part of the overall service that a company provides.

Develop a written job description for each position. Including yours. A job description describes the knowledge, experience, and abilities required for each position, as well as the specific tasks, responsibilities, and expected outcomes. This document allows new employees to settle in quickly and provides a gauge to measure performance. You should write or be involved in the development of each job plan. Review and update them as needed every twelve to twenty-four months or as positions change. Pass out companywide job descriptions to all employees. Include a shortened version with subs' and clients' contracts to help them understand the company structure.[30]

A group of people connected by a common vision is a powerful thing. Therefore, actively build a team atmosphere by encouraging social interaction (daily social connections, company trips, picnics, sports), group training, and even professional team-building exercises if money allows.[31] The sense of being part of a team—a group that respects and trusts each other and shares a common vision—makes work meaningful and more productive; it forms bonds that encourage better communication resulting in a better product; it helps to identify and use the strengths of each member; and it demands personal growth that benefits both the individual and the company.

> Your most precious possession is not your financial assets. …[it] is the people you have working there, and what they carry around in their heads, and their ability to work together. —Robert Reich

---

30 Find sample job descriptions on the web and in trade magazines.

31 There are organizations that run team-building exercises.

Hiring

Employment at a construction company appeals to people from all walks of life. Many folks are not interested in a college degree or have one and dislike their field. The building business is appealing because it offers hands-on work, good compensation, and a team atmosphere.

Before deciding to hire new staff ask these questions: Is there an unmistakable need for the position? Can existing staff handle it? Will it be profitable? Should this item be subcontracted or a consultant brought in? Each new position requires resources, training, and increased overhead. Hire only after carefully considering other options.

Don't hire a full-time person for a part-time position hoping for more work in the future.

Decide if you need a skilled person or someone you can train. A skilled person will cost more but will quickly produce results and will need little more than orientation to company procedures. An unskilled person will cost less, can be trained to do things your way, and is often more flexible than a highly skilled person, but they need intense supervision and training. Balance the benefits and weaknesses of each approach against the requirements of the position.

Always do a criminal background check when hiring a position that will handle money. Regardless of how long you have known a candidate or who recommended them, check their background. Spend extra time talking with references and search online for information about the applicant.

Put substantial effort into your hiring interviews. Select a few of the most promising applicants and then have one or two people join you in the interview process. As a group you will see more and these insights will be invaluable in making the right hire. Ask each applicant the same questions, keeping notes of their answers and your impressions. Give each person a fair chance at the job; many tradesmen have the values and abilities required but can't talk about them easily. Call every reference. If after going through the hiring process no one seems to be right, start again. Put in the effort to hire the right person now rather than suffering the consequences of a poor choice later on.

———————

In my experience the slickest talker is usually the poorest worker.

———————

Draw out potential employees or subcontractors during the interviews. Be on time. Be polite. Do not chat. Do not be overly friendly and don't try to be funny. Before the meeting prepare a list of questions and begin the interview with the easy ones. Make them comfortable and get them to talk. Encourage them to articulate their own ideas and don't ask questions in a way that directs the answer. Listen carefully. Repeat questions to which you did not understand the answer. Interviewing is an important skill that is learned and refined through practice.

———————

Companies cannot legally say much about former employees. Federal laws and the possibility of being sued limit what companies can say about past employees. The worst and most contentious employees are the most dangerous to be honest about. Some people, if they feel confident that the information will not go beyond you, will be honest anyway.

———————

Learn to discern phony references. Some people give friends and family as references if they have a limited or bad work history. But people giving false information have no depth to their story and if you ask enough questions and listen closely you will know if what they are saying is true. Also, when people actually have something to say they elaborate on their ideas and at some point it will be clear that the information is real.

Do not persuade or force someone to fit into the wrong position. Accept that some people have neither the ability nor the interest in taking on certain roles. There is no point in losing a good tradesman because you push him into being a foreman when supervision, customer service, or scheduling is beyond his interest or grasp.

> "Everyone is a genius. But if you judge a fish by
> its ability to climb a tree, it will live its whole life
> believing that it is stupid." —Albert Einstein

Consider hiring a company runner. It is incredibly helpful to have someone who gets materials, goes to the bank, brings tools to the jobs, picks up permits, and does anything as required. Besides allowing field and office staff to concentrate on their job, a runner offers a quick nondisruptive response to problems. Hire a smart, motivated individual—active retirees work well—and he will become a critical part of the company as his knowledge of company personnel and suppliers grows.

Hire people with more skill and experience than you have. They will help you and the organization improve.

> "You can do some things and you can't do other
> things. Don't get upset about the things you can't
> do. If you can't do something, pay someone else
> who can…" —Jim Paul

If you consistently make bad hires, assess your process. You may not be giving the hiring process enough attention, you may be avoiding choosing the best people for personal reasons, or the company or your manner may be turning them away. Review your hiring process and learn to do it differently or consider hiring a consultant to help choose employees.

———————

Hire all employees on a trial basis of from one to three months. Hiring this way helps in assessing new employees without making a commitment to them.[32] During the trial period you test each other out; they, to see if they like the work and the company, and you, to appraise their skill and learn if they fit. During the trial period you may let them go for any reason, but when they are officially hired, the company assumes the legal obligations that every employer has for its employees.

———————

If you find someone extraordinary, try to find a spot for them. People who are exceptional at what they do are rare. If you encounter someone whose talents fit your company's needs but you don't have a current opening, consider creating one. But follow the standard hiring procedures and be certain that your overhead can support the position.

———————

Do not hire people who constantly complain and are angry at the world. Their attitude damages them and everyone around them.

> "I have never met a successful pessimist."
> —William O'Neil

———————

32 Basic employment rights such as being paid, safe working conditions, and not being discriminated against remain unchanged and even the on-trial employee may file a grievance based on these issues.

Be thoughtful when hiring a friend or family member. Often the expectations in hiring someone close to you—loyalty, trust, compatibility—don't work out. Regardless of who the candidate is, follow company hiring procedure and choose the best fit. If the friend or family member is the right person, hire them, but talk through potential problems in advance, set up boundaries, and write down and sign what is agreed to. This will give the arrangement more chance of succeeding and provide a basis for ending their employment if necessary.

Employee Relations

Running a company is by definition a team effort. As its leader your most important tasks are direction (vision/goals), organization (systems/efficiency), and communication (information/education).

> "To believe in yourself and to follow your dreams,
>   to have goals in life and a drive to succeed, and
>   to surround yourself with the things and the
>   people that make you happy—this is success!"
> —Sasha Azevedo

You cannot overcommunicate. This holds true for employees, subcontractors, suppliers, and customers; everyone wants to know what is happening now and in the future. To say that you can't overcommunicate is not to say that you can't overwhelm people with mountains of irrelevant information. Convey the important stuff succinctly and share it often with everyone.

> "Communication is the real work of leadership."
> —Nitin Nohria

Notice, compliment, and reward behavior that matches the company's goals and expectations.

Understand what is reasonable to expect from employees. When starting out, it's difficult to know. Here are some ideas: honesty, active participation, speaking well of coworkers and the company in public and private, neat dress, organized and safe job sites, being on time, taking care of tools and equipment, and treating coworkers and clients with respect. It is not reasonable to expect them to work as hard as you do, to do things exactly as you would, to live for the company, or not to make mistakes.

The best employees have high expectations. If you want to keep those employees, those expectations are nonnegotiable: being honest and reliable, paying on time and competitively, having a reward system, providing a steady flow of good work, having (or learning) good management skills, having competent and affable co-workers, providing and enforcing companywide rules, providing or facilitating training and education, and providing a vision of the company's future and by extension that of the individual within the company.

> "Setting an example is not the main means
> of influencing another, it is the only means."
> —Albert Einstein

Let relationships with new employees develop. As you get to know each other, learn what they can do, if they make sound decisions, and if they are trustworthy. Only as they prove their ability should their responsibilities and authority increase.

Training is often just as important as money to self-motivated employees. Training may be done in-house using your own people, from books and trade publications, at workshops or conferences, and at technical schools and colleges. The National Association of The Remodeling Industry (NARI) and the National Association of Home Builders (NAHB) both offer training programs[33].

Look for mentors in your company. If someone is a good teacher and he is willing, have him formally mentor others. If he is exceptional at it, think about creating a part-time position in which he has a formal teaching role.

Encourage employees to continue their education, both in their trade and personally. For key people, do what you can to accommodate and pay for some or all of that training.

> "Education is the movement from darkness to light."
> —Allan Bloom

People who don't make mistakes aren't doing anything. Create an atmosphere in which honest mistakes are lessons used to improve one's abilities and then forgotten. If people are belittled or punished for mistakes they won't work as hard or take initiative and the best will quit.

> "You can be discouraged by failure—or you can
> learn from it. So go ahead and make mistakes.
> Make all you can. Because, remember, that's where
> you will find success." —Thomas J. Watson

---

33 Both organizations have local chapters and a large online presence.

Second guessing, anger, or intimidation will undermine employees' confidence. Just like with children, they will become unable or unwilling to take initiative. The most effective ones will leave, and the ones who remain will need direction for the simplest tasks.

———————

Most people are inherently good. They want a place to express their talent, to belong, and to do good work. And most of us will put extraordinary effort into an organization that encourages creativity and participation.

———————

Gainsharing measures productivity and rewards the employee or subcontractor for increased yield on a specific project. For example, if a framing sub bids $10,000 to frame a house and the framing crew does the work for $8000, with gainsharing the framing crew would be given a percentage of the $2000 saving.

———————

Offer creative incentives besides money. Examples are flexible hours, coming in early or working late, four ten-hours-a-day workweeks,[34] or, for office staff—if their job allows—working some time at home.[35]

———————

Learn to delegate tasks and authority and get out of the way. When delegating it is your responsibility to communicate the intended outcome clearly, for the task and within the broader company goals. With those you know and trust, once you have assigned a task, let them do it their way. People have more com-mitment when they are in charge of the process and the result.

———————

34 A four ten-hours-a-day workweek may actually save the company money and, in my experience, customers and employees like it a lot.

35 Begin allowing people to work at home on a trial basis and only those you trust completely. It takes a certain kind of person to remain focused— that is, not to screw around—while working at home.

Implement profit sharing. Most of us, knowing that part of a company's profit will translate into a personal reward, are motivated to increase those earnings. The more tangible the results we experience the more engaged we are. Profit sharing may be paid in the form of cash, education, day care, healthcare, vacation, tools, a truck, fuel, company gatherings or trips, or a more formal savings or retirement plan. Profit sharing may be based on the owner's whim or on a complex formula. But because of the cyclical nature of building, the complexity of project accounting, and the need to be fair to employees and the company, these plans are harder to implement and administer than one would expect. There are companies that sell and administer profit-sharing plans.[36] Their advantage is that you don't have to invent a system: they have various formulas to choose from, they take on the fiduciary and administrative responsibility, and the plan can be put into place quickly. Whatever plan you buy or create, research the subject carefully, understand the options, and be certain that it is flexible enough to adjust or suspend payment as profit fluctuates. Although it is important to be generous, the company must have enough working capital and profit to function and grow; don't give away too much.

> "Start with good people, lay out the rules, communicate with your employees, motivate them and reward them. If you do all these things effectively, you can't miss". —Lee Iacocca

---

36 Search the web for a "third-party administrator of profit sharing plans." There are large and small companies. Thoroughly understand what they offer and don't buy more than you need.

Remind employees of benefits from profit sharing and other perks. List their personal benefits on their paycheck and show collective benefits in companywide communications. Over time people begin to think of benefits and perks as entitlements, and therefore it is important to remind them that these items are added benefits—not regular pay—and that they may fluctuate or be eliminated depending on personal performance and company financial health. Also, when people consider what they are paid, they often don't include less obvious compensation. Regular reminders could help keep people around.

Create an atmosphere that encourages employees to stay; but understand some will leave anyway. People move, get sick, change jobs, or leave to start a business. Do what you can to get people to stay, but support what is best for them. The advantages are that you will have advance notice before someone leaves, you may be able to negotiate to get them to stay, they will speak well of the company, they may become an excellent sub, or, because they left on good terms, they may return to work for you in the future. Also, the opening could be a chance for fresh talent to reorganize and strengthen the area of the business that the previous employee left.

Firing

Understand applicable rules for firing employees. In the 1970s and '80s the idea that an employer could fire an employee "at will," that is, for any reason or no reason, began to change as new laws were passed.[37] Because of these new laws in some situations employees may sue for wrongful termination. This generally applies to larger companies, but there are many examples of it affecting small ones.[38] Unfortunately the rules are poorly defined, erratic in interpretation and execution, change over time, and are different from state to state.[39] Therefore, determine what applies to your company by contacting local authorities, checking the web, and, perhaps, speaking with a labor attorney. It could be that without clear and documented reasons for the firing, you will need to make an effort to have an employee correct the problem and to document that effort—and only then, fire them—or it could be that you can still fire "at will."

When firing someone have at least one other person in the room. If there are threats or physical violence, you will need help to stop it and witnesses in case the police are called in. And don't fire someone in your office. You want to be able to leave the meeting and return to your office if they won't stop arguing about the decision.

------

37 See the Model Employment Termination Act (META) for some help in this matter. META is not a law, but it offers guidelines that may help determine what a fair dismissal is.

38 As of this writing (2013), employers with fewer than five employees may still fire "at will," but check to be certain that this remains true.

39 For example, as of this writing, Pennsylvania remains an "at will" state, while California has more, and more complex rules than a rational person would think possible.

Despite your best effort, some employees will not work out. It may be difficult to define the issue: poor attitude, slow work, deceitfulness, not getting along with others, blaming, or having an excuse for every problem. Many people will justify themselves endlessly, causing more uncertainty. I tried countless times to help marginal employees, but it never worked. My inclination now is to let people go quickly.[40] But because hiring and training is costly, because there may be legal issues, and because it often seems that something should help, you may decide to work with an employee in an attempt to correct the problem. If so, begin by interviewing them to understand their point of view and to explain yours.[41] From that meeting, detail the problems and the changes required in a letter, formally ask the employee to make these changes, have them sign the letter to acknowledge that they understand what is required and agree to make the changes. Allow a reasonable amount of time, but set a date by which the changes must be made. If they do not make the changes, both in fact and in the spirit of what is expected, let them go. Document every step along the way without embellishment: the issues, meetings, conversations, and efforts to help them succeed.

---

40 This is partly a function of size. While a large organization may have the in-house expertise and resources to work with problem employees, a small company will not, and one bad employee can cause serious damage.

41 Have at least one other person involved in the entire process to get an additional perspective and for backup should it become a legal issue.

You will have employees whom you trust who violate that trust. They may steal, cheat, or lie. It might even be someone you consider a friend. Fire them quickly and take the appropriate legal action but do not dwell on it or get involved in reprisals or revenge; this will increase the damage. You will be deeply disappointed each time it happens, but the answer is not to stop trusting. It could be time to improve existing systems to catch problems sooner or to improve hiring procedures. But mostly, you have to accept that sometimes people do bad things and that the best response is to let it go and move on. And don't take it personally. Even though many people justify their bad behavior by blaming it on others, it is about their choices and actions, not you.

> "Never argue with a fool; onlookers may not be able to tell the difference." —Mark Twain

SUBCONTRACTOR

Subcontractor or Sub is any individual or company that works under a "subcontract" to the General Contractor's primary contract. Subs provide their area of expertise and agree to abide by the GC's time schedule and other job requirements.

Good subs answer their phone or return calls promptly; they are smart and engaged in their work; they are interested in your project and if not they let you know quickly; they do what they say when they say, and they let you know when issues arise; they are confident, not arrogant or self-important; they hire, train, and keep competent employees; they provide a comprehensive contract and scope-of-work (if you don't); they provide timely and accurate bids and invoices; they keep licenses and insurance policies up to date; they meet job schedules; they keep their supplies and equipment organized; they quickly and fairly resolve problems; and they work amiably with other subs and the customer. Skilled subs cost more because running a well-ordered company is more expensive than running a shoddy one.

Bad subs tend to cost less initially but far more in aggravation, dollars, and damage to your reputation as the inevitable problems arise. A sub represents your company in exactly the same way that employees do—customers may not even know they are not employees.

Subcontractors have advantages over employees: they are responsible for and warranty their own work; they are not entitled to unemployment benefits or workman's compensation; they are not eligible for company benefits or perks; they have expertise, equipment, or licenses that you don't; and you hire them only when you need them. Every project may be subcontracted fully or in part, and each GC chooses which parts to do with employees and which to do with subs based on the budget, the availability and skill of employees, the job requirements, and the amount of work coming up.[42]

It takes time and effort to build relationships with a group of competent, reliable, and fairly priced subs and such a list of good subs is one of a builder's most important assets. The more professional you are in keeping appointments, supplying thorough job documents, fair contracts, paying on time, treating them with respect, and scheduling so they can start on time, the easier it will be to find and retain the best ones.

"…I remind myself that my inner and outer life depend on the labours of other men, living and dead, and that I must exert myself in order to give in the same measure as I have received."
—Albert Einstein

---

42 In residential construction, individual trades are less likely than a GC to sub work out; however, all companies will do it if they have an especially large project or if they have an overwhelming workload.

SUBCONTRACTOR NOTES

Finding Subs

Find good subs by asking other builders and at supply houses. If you are a member of a local building association, it will have a list of recommended folks. Look online, take numbers off job signs and company trucks, and look in the "trades and services" section of your local paper's classified ads or on Craigslist for small specialty trades. Regardless of how highly someone is recommended, call references, look at their work, and write tight specifications and contracts.

Be certain the sub has experience with the type of work you need done. Having worked on new homes does not necessarily mean that they have the same level of skill with restoration or small commercial work.

It may take persistence to get better subs to bid with you at first. When contacting a new sub to bid on a job, you may find them reluctant. Better subs focus on companies they already know, they are busy, and they are regularly approached by companies that take up their time and don't provide work. For these reasons, you may need to convince them that bidding with you will be worth their time.

As a company grows the subs it uses will need to grow too. Some will, others won't try, and still others will try but fail to keep up with what is required. For this reason, as you make a decision to grow the company, form relationships with larger subs in each trade and with varying capacity so that if one can't do what is required you know others who can.

Consider the different qualities of smaller and bigger subcontractors. Smaller companies tend to be more flexible, less expensive, more concerned about keeping your business, more creative, and often better performers than their larger counterparts. They can also disappear quickly, have fewer assets to go after if required, and have less capacity to do different types of work, and, if there are problems, it may be more about the owner's personality than the issues. Large companies have more resources and capacity, can respond quicker, have a deeper pool of talent, and will be around if there are problems. They can also be more bureaucratic and more expensive because of higher overhead, and, if there are legal issues, they have more resources to make your life difficult.

Avoid using subs you've had problems with. When a new job is starting, and past problems are forgotten, you may be tempted to reuse a marginal sub because it is easier than finding a new one. Don't. Find a better sub.

Be careful about hiring an unknown sub who shows up on a job site offering to start work quickly. They may be a good sub needing work or a poor sub trying to avoid the normal selection process. If they are a good sub, it could work out well for both of you, but don't allow their availability or your need, to abort the vetting process or to allow work to begin without written specifications and a contract.

Understand the pluses and minuses of exclusively using subs. Some companies have no tradesmen working in the field, using subs to do all of their work, with superintendents managing the jobs. This approach has advantages and disadvantages— lower overhead, but less direct control of the work, for example. Consider all sides before choosing to work in this way.[43]

------

43 See "Subbing Out Everything," February 1999, *The Journal of Light Construction,* for a detailed account of one company that handles work in this way.

Bidding

You don't always need to get three bids. Industry lore says to get three bids for every trade on every project, but on small to mid-sized jobs and those that need to begin quickly (water or fire damage, for example), this is often impractical: the job is too small to interest subs, getting bids takes more time than it's worth, or the bidding process pushes the start date too far away. The alternatives are either to have relationships with subs you trust and use them on a less formal basis—time and materials, cost-plus, or a ballpark estimate, for example—or to learn to estimate for the trades on small projects.[44]

Ask subs and suppliers to submit their preliminary pricing figures in writing. This includes "best guess," "ball park," "rule-of-thumb," and "rough estimates." Committing their prices to paper makes them real numbers, that is, figures they will honor if the job happens. Further, having prices in writing will save you from using too low a number in a preliminary estimate, or worse, the bid. Also, know that as a project's details are clarified or changed during the bidding process the sub's and supplier's pricing may also change.

Bids from qualified subs can help assess the project. Subs have the ability to find trade-related problems—things overlooked, badly designed, or not meeting codes, for example—when they visit the job or review job documents to produce their estimate.

---

44 HomeTech Publishing's estimating system provides quick, fairly accurate bids for most of the trades you will use. But estimating other trades is tricky: bid too high and you won't get the work; bid too low and you will pay the difference between your estimated cost and the actual cost of the work. One alternative is to develop a feel for trade pricing by repeatedly doing estimates for trades on which you have bids coming in and compare your pricing with these bids. Another is to have trades that you trust and work from their prices.

Let subs know that you are getting other bids. It will help keep their bid in line.

———————

Every sub's bid must include furnishing *all* material, labor, taxes, and permits required to complete their work. That is, everything historically associated with that trade must be provided for in the bid price.

———————

It's okay for a sub to reuse a bid. You may find that a sub has already bid a project with another GC, and they use the same bid with you. There is nothing wrong with this practice and it will save you time.

———————

Review incoming bids and ask enough questions to be certain they are complete. If an unknown sub bids too low—either by mistake or intentionally—when the work begins, they will skimp on something or paper the job with change orders.

———————

It is reasonable to expect a sub's price for the same work to be less to a GC than to a homeowner, in part, because the GC will provide repeat business.

———————

Price—although not the only concern—does matter. Competition among subs is the best way to assure that you are not overpaying.[45] Therefore develop and maintain relationships with a few subs in each trade so that you get competitive bids and you are not hamstrung by dependence on any one sub.

———————

45 There are some alternatives—learning to estimate different trades in-house or paying other subs for estimates to check pricing—but each has downsides and neither offers a better long-term solution than competitive bidding on jobs large enough to warrant getting bids.

Subs vary in their pricing strategies. Some will give competitive prices over and over again for years; some will inch their way higher with each job; some always give high prices; and some will regularly give astronomically high prices with the hope of getting one every so often.

————————

Watch for signs of financial problems. When interviewing trades, if you listen carefully you may hear that the sub is having financial problems: if they ask for too much up front or if they are overly concerned with when they get paid. They may come right out and say that they are short on cash. It may still be okay to use them if everything else checks out, but make it clear that you strictly follow the terms of payment as detailed in the contract—and do that.

————————

Bids from subs of different sizes are often not directly comparable. Small subs will often win on price (their overhead is lower) but they will have less capacity and expertise to produce a large job while large subs can sometimes be too expensive for small projects.

————————

Don't hire on a "gut feeling." Whether it is because you need someone to start quickly, you are too busy, or you believe that you "read" people well, hiring in this way will significantly increase the number of problems you face. Allow time to follow a vetting procedure: call references, notice their organization, examine their work, review your company contract and other requirements with them, and ask lots of questions.

————————

Develop a procedure to inform subs when they win a contract. If you say or even imply that a sub has won a contract, you may have verbally agreed to give them the work and, depending on the circumstances, that agreement may be legally binding, or at the very least, it will cause friction if you decide not to give it to them. To avoid this, follow a procedure of reviewing bids for each job in-house to decide which sub to use, and then, in a consistent manner—phone, letter, or email—inform the successful bidders that they have won the contract.

If you are asked to bid for a large GC, be wary. It is fairly common for big GCs to include little or no profit in their bid and then figuratively beat their profit out of subs using contract terms favorable to them, back charges, or vague specifications allowing excessive demands. They get away with this because often small subs don't understand the terms of the contract they sign and once involved in the project they have little choice except to go along because they don't have the resources to dispute issues, the GC is holding money, suing is costly and rarely pays, and walking away opens them to lawsuits. Therefore, carefully study the contract and specifications—*understand every clause*—review the contract with your lawyer,[46] and modify or insert your own clauses and specifications to protect your rights. If possible call subs the GC uses—try to talk with subs not currently working for them, those who are may not be forthcoming about problems—and ask about how the company treats them.

Be considerate of unsuccessful bidders. When the bidding is over and the subs are selected, respect the effort of the folks who did not win the bid by letting them know the outcome and thanking them for their time. Besides being the right thing to do, it makes it more likely they will bid your next project.

---

46 This is the time to have a lawyer with extensive construction experience, not one who needs to read up on the subject.

Contracts

Have a contract and use change orders with every sub, every time. Each time that you choose not to do this because you know the sub or you're in a hurry or they came highly recommended, and things go badly, you will be reminded yet again why contracts and change orders are essential.

———————

Include a clause in every sub's contract stating that they will not be paid until you have a valid certificate of insurance from their insurance company. Require that the insurance company mail the certificate directly to you; subs have been known to forge them or to alter the dates. Check the dates that the policy is in force to be certain it covers the time that the sub will be working with you. If you have doubts, call the insurer to confirm that the information is correct.

———————

In every subs' contracts include a list of types of insurance they are required to carry. Include the dollar limit for each one and require that the policy include your company as *an additional insured*. This will indemnify you against the sub's mistakes. Talk with your insurance agent to better understand the current thinking on this issue and the reasons for requiring subs to indemnify your company.

———————

Contractually require subs to obtain, pay for, and comply with all permits and inspections. And require each sub to meet their trade's inspector on-site if someone must be present. If you or a foreman are going to be there, you might do the sub a favor and meet the inspector, but as standard procedure the trade is responsible for meeting inspectors and taking care of any issues that arise from the inspection.

———————

Put in all subs' contracts that, when possible, they will keep the same tradesmen on a job from start to finish. Including call backs and warranty work. The contract should also require that the sub confers with you before changing crews. But know that such consistency is not always possible: people take vacations, get sick, are fired, or quit, and some trades require different crews for different stages of their work.

––––––––––

Negotiate a "draw" or payment schedule with each sub. Incremental payments based on the progress of the work are standard. In negotiating this schedule, the subs are trying to get money as early as possible to increase their cash flow and to lessen their exposure should there be problems, while the GC is trying to keep cash for operations and to maintain leverage on the subs if problems arise.

––––––––––

Extras will not be paid for unless approved by change order (CO). State this policy in the bid documents and contract. Each CO must detail the extra work, its cost, and the amount of time it will add to the schedule. If there is a dispute, the CO will provide documentation, but also by defining and tracking what was agreed to, you will avoid conflict. The contract should also define who will create the CO, the sub or the GC.

––––––––––

Licenses & Insurance

Know which trades are required to have licenses in your area. Ask all subcontractors to provide you with copies of their licenses. If there is any reason to doubt a sub, call the agency to be sure the document is valid. Having a license indicates a sub has met the *minimum requirements*. It is not an indication of quality of work, ability, or financial health.[47]

Get a W-9 form from all subs for identification purposes. That form includes their Taxpayer Identification Number (TIN), which is either their Employer Identification Number (EIN) or their Social Security (SS) number.

Be aware of the rules that distinguish subs from employees. Subs set their own hours, own their tools and equipment, make profit or loss from their work, own the business entity under which they provide services, have control over the performance of their work, have the ability to hire employees to perform the work, maintain a business location, maintain liability insurance, and have a signed contract between parties. Not all of these standards must be met—you can lend a sub tools or set the hours that a site may be worked on, and there is no legal requirement to have a contract—but the more of these rules that apply, the easier it will be to prove the sub is not an employee. [48]

---

[47] See www.contractors-license.org for an overview by state of license requirements. This site has other valuable information as well.

[48] Both state and federal laws may apply. State rules may vary, so check the laws in the state where the work is to be performed.

Understand the state and federal tax laws for employees and subs and follow them.[49] Businesses sometimes list employees as subs when filing state and federal taxes because there is significantly less cost and paper work—no workman's compensation and no unemployment benefits, for example— but there are severe penalties for misclassifying workers. When caught the company will be required to pay all of the charges they would have paid for each misclassified employee retroactively, plus interest and penalties. The resulting costs have put many companies out of business.

———————

Do not carry subs under your insurance. GCs sometimes cover small subs under their insurance, charging the sub what the GC would pay for the subs insurance. There are several downsides to this arrangement:

- It opens you to possible long-term liabilities, including claims for long-term care or rehabilitation if a sub is injured.

- The cost of insuring the sub will be included in next year's premium whether you use them again or not.

- The trade rate for the sub may be higher than your workers' rate, and it may raise your company's overall rate.

- The sub may pick up help, adding more liability and cost.

49 Read *Hiring Independent Contractors, The Employer's Legal Guide,* by S. Fishman, also review articles in *The Journal of Light Construction* and see *A Contractor's Guide to Construction Law,* by Q. Behler.

- You may figure the rate wrong, or the subs' trade rate may go up, and you would pay significantly more for their insurance than you charged them.

- Because you supplied the subs insurance, they could be considered employees by state and federal tax authorities, subjecting you to an employee's labor burden for the sub.

- When found out, the insurance company may insist on charging for the sub's entire invoice not just the labor portion.[50]

- It could void your insurance policy.

_____

Get a certificate of insurance (CI) from every sub before they begin work.[51] A CI is a letter issued by the sub's insurance company that certifies they have insurance coverage—usually workman's compensation and general liability—the dollar amount that will be covered in the event of an incident, and the time period that the insurance will be in force. It names your company as a "certificate holder" and it includes the name of the insurance company providing coverage.

- If subs do not have insurance and they are hurt on your job, your rates will skyrocket because your insurance will be forced to cover their claim.

_____

50 The insurance company has no way of knowing if an invoice claims less labor and more material than was actually used and therefore they may charge it all as labor.

51 If, for whatever reason, you don't get a CI before the work begins, hold payment until you have one in hand. If it turns out that they don't have insurance have them leave the job immediately and either get the CI before they return or terminate their contact. If they have begun work, consider taking your costs for disruption to the job out of what you owe them.

- Because your insurance company does an annual audit of your books—all payment and payroll records—to verify that they have charged for everyone for whom they could have paid a claim and for each sub from whom you don't have a CI, you will pay for them as if they were your employee. *This will be expensive.* Your "general liability" rate will rise because it is based on payroll. Your current year payroll rate will rise based on the amount you paid the sub.[52] Your future rates will rise based on the higher payroll, and depending on the trade of the uninsured sub—roofers and tree trimmers rates are far higher than carpenters for example—your overall rate will be adjusted upward. *Therefore, require a CI from every sub and check to be sure that the coverage amount and dates are correct to cover the jobs they will work on.*[53]

- Most insurance companies send a notice of cancellation if a sub terminates or loses their insurance, and generally they will send a new certificate when it is updated or renewed. *But they accept no liability for not doing so.* Require that the certificate is sent directly to you from the insurance company so that it cannot be falsified and track the expiration dates on the CI.

- The single exception to getting a CI is the sub who works alone or in a partnership that has no employees and therefore does not need to carry

---

52 The insurance company charges are for labor only; however, if the subs invoice does not detail labor and material—many don't—you will be charged as if the entire bill were labor.

53 Ask your insurance agent what the standard amount of coverage is. Also, some jobs require coverage that is higher than the standard. The amount will be detailed in the job specifications.

workers' compensation insurance;[54] he must still provide a CI for liability insurance however. In this situation, ask him for an 'Independent Contractors Statement' (ICS), which states that he is not entitled to workers' compensation coverage from your insurance.[55]

Managing Subs

Schedule subs sequentially. It is generally better to have the HVAC rough in first, then the plumber, and then the electrician because it is easier for the plumber to work around the HVAC lines and for the electrician to run their work around both of them.

Talk with the key trades when developing a project schedule because they are more likely to meet dates they were involved in setting. Send project updates because it will allow them to adjust their schedule as the project dates change, and it will remind them of what they agreed to.

Allow subs to use the material and methods they are comfortable with, as long as it does not compromise quality or the job specifications. This will generally cost less, the finished product will be better, and the job will move faster.

54 Both state and federal laws may apply. State rules may vary, so check the laws in the state where the work is to be performed.

55 This varies from state to state and over time. Check with your insurance agent and local authorities to understand the rules in the area in which you work.

Avoid paying subs before their work begins.[56] This is especially true if you have not used them before. Many will ask for their first payment at the contract signing to increase their cash flow and to protect themselves. If a sub you don't know well but want to use insists on being paid at contract signing instead of at the completion of the first phase of work, offer to pay the day they begin work. At that point at least they have shown up and have material on-site.

Use an abbreviated version of the company employee policy manual for subs. A subcontractor represents your company in the same way an employee does—in many cases the client will not know if they are an employee or a sub—therefore they must be held to the same standards as employees. Make the manual a legal addendum to their contract, review it with new subs, and have them sign it to acknowledge receipt, understanding, and agreement.[57]

The bulk of a job's information is passed along through specifications and blue prints, but excellence is in the details and the foreman must make clear to subs—diplomatically when possible, forcefully when necessary—what needs to be done to meet the unwritten but essential requirements of quality, neatness, and cooperation.

---

56 There are exceptions: if a substantial deposit is required because specialty materials or supplies must be ordered and paid for in advance, you may need to pay before work begins. If you have doubts about the sub, pay the supplier directly, although the sub is likely to be offended by your mistrust.

57 The subs abbreviated manual is intended to spell out basic job standards— no swearing or smoking in the house, for example—but it cannot dictate direction or control the subs' work because controlling their own work is a key part of what makes them a legal subcontractor. Have your lawyer review the subcontractors' manual to be certain it complies with the law.

When trade-related issues arise, ask subs for their opinion and suggestions. You hired them for their skill and knowledge, so listen to their perspective and then decide how to proceed. But do not abdicate, even to the best subs, responsibility for decisions that affect the quality, the appearance, or the job schedule.

> "A GC who lets his subs run the job is never a good thing." —Dick Morse

---

Some good subs have idiosyncrasies. They are grumpy, disorganized, work odd hours, or have a strange sense of humor. It can sometimes be worth working with them anyway. This notion contradicts what has been said about good subs being well organized, but there are folks who seem as scattered as a dust cloud but end up producing great work. If they manage to keep a tight rein in the field it is often the business—billing, taxes, insurance—that suffers, so if you decide to use them watch these issues closely as they affect your company.

Require subs to include in their contract the hourly labor rate and the material mark-up rate that they will use in their change orders.[58] If these numbers are not agreed to in advance, subs are in a position to charge pretty much anything they want for extras. If their initial figures are too high, negotiate for a better rate.

In the contract, require subs to broom clean their work area and at the end of each day to put their trash in the job site dumpster. Job site dumpsters are typically provided by the GC.

---

58 See "Sample, subcontractor Agreement" in the Appendix.

You cannot force performance from incompetent or unwilling subs. There will be times that a sub is not performing well—off-schedule, marginal quality, or poor job behavior—but unless they are grossly incompetent—that is, they are caught stealing or drunk or the quality of their work is absurd—the contract will not allow you to toss them off the job.[59] Speak with your lawyer to understand your options. You could force them to leave, although this may seriously disrupt the budget and schedule, and they may sue for breach of contract. You might compel them to improve by holding money or threatening legal action, but you can't get blood from a stone. In some cases, if there is enough money and it does not damage the job too much, you may be able to buy out their contract for a portion of the full amount and replace them with a better sub. If their work is marginally acceptable, it may be best, while pushing for improvement, to allow them to complete their work. There is no easy answer, only your best effort to work through a bad situation and to avoid it in the future.

The GC must be told when a sub is planning to subcontract some or all of his work. In some cases, although not often in residential work, there are sub-subs. That is, a company acting as a subcontractor to the subcontractor who signed the original contract with the GC. The second sub is brought in to do some or all of the work because the first sub is too busy or the project is too large or too specialized for them to handle alone. In every case the GC must be told of this arrangement beforehand and given a chance to approve, disapprove, or modify the agreement.

---

59 Deal with every problem directly and immediately and increase your normal job documentation when issues arise; if it becomes a legal matter the documentation will be invaluable.

Do not make the final payment to a sub until the work is inspected. *EVER*. When a dozen things are clamoring for attention, and a small sub reports their work is complete and payment is due, it is easy to pay the bill, only to find out later that the work is incomplete or poorly done.

_____

Note changes in subs' performance from job to job. Companies, like people, change over time. Therefore, even with your most trusted subs, notice if their quality or service declines. If it does, point it out to them and ask that they correct the problem. If they can't or won't, think about changing subs.

_____

Build off-the-job relationships with your best subs. Take them out to lunch once in a while and invite them to company functions.

_____

Keep key subs informed about company changes. When your company faces issue such as an economic slowdown, policy changes, changes in the type of jobs pursued, or safety issues, meet with your key subs, either individually or as a group, to let them know what you are planning and how it might affect them.

_____

SUPPLIERS

A company selling supplies and equipment.

A distributor of products to the end user.

A wholesale supplier, in theory, sells products only to professional business customers, but many will sell to anyone who walks in the door.

Suppliers, like subs, are an important part of a builder's success. With each supplier you are looking for the best combination of inventory, service, knowledge, timely delivery, competitive prices, and quick and fair handling of problems. Using the best suppliers will make you a better builder.

For large orders—lumber, paint, electrical, roofing, drywall materials, for example—use supply houses instead of box stores because their quality and service is better; they have deeper inventory and more technical expertise and product information; they deliver; and often their prices for equivalent items are the same or lower than the box stores. Box stores may save time when picking up odds and ends or searching for the solution to a problem because of their varied inventory, but for the bulk of your business, specialty stores are better.[60]

When considering using new suppliers, visit the stores, check the inventory, and ask for lists of what they carry and their pricing. Look at their selection of product literature and catalogs. Ask what they keep in stock and how long it generally takes to get not-in-stock items. What is their policy on in-stock and special order returns? Do they deliver and generally how quickly and for how big an order? Can you call

---

60 Box stores sometimes appear to be selling a similar product for less when they aren't. Differences may be impossible to see until the item is used or thoroughly researched—cheaper steel, lower grade lumber, fewer ply's, lower voltage—differences that are missed by many of us. Generally, industry suppliers assume that a professional wants to use the best products available and they screen them so that you don't have too.

in an order and have it ready when you get there? How fast is the in-store service? Choose the most knowledgeable salesman to work with. What is their discount policy? What are their payment terms?[61]

"The great successful men of the world have
used their imaginations, they think ahead and
create their mental picture, and then go to work
materializing that picture in all its details, filling
in here, adding a little there, altering this a bit and
that bit, but steadily building, steadily building."
—Robert Collier

61 Some stores give a 2% discount if you pay within ten days of the purchase date. This is called "net thirty," which means that you can take thirty days to pay the bill, but you don't get the 2% discount.

SUPPLIER NOTES

Selecting Suppliers

Different businesses require different things from their suppliers, and suppliers tend to develop specialties. A high-production new-home builder buys on a large scale and is generally more interested in price and delivery than service. A smaller volume but high-end new-home builder is looking for excellent products and service. Remodelers are searching for solutions and hard-to-find items and, therefore, require a varied inventory and product knowledge. They tend to be less concerned with cost. A custom cabinetmaker is more concerned with an excellent and varied supply of wood and hardware.

Look for family-owned businesses. They typically offer better service and product knowledge and sell higher quality products because, quite literally, their business survival depends on it.

Loyalty to a few good suppliers has important advantages. They will give priority service, deliver consistent product, and to some extent, watch out for your interests.

Meet with your key suppliers to negotiate pricing. This will save a great deal of time because you won't need to constantly check prices. Periodically confirm that their prices remain competitive. With suppliers you use only occasionally, always check prices.

Be certain you are getting trade prices. Some suppliers sell to builders at trade prices and some at retail—that is, the same price that a homeowner pays. Establish accounts at stores that give trade discounts and review them at least once a year. Some supply houses sell only (or mostly) to the trades and their marked prices have the discounts already built in—plumbing and roofing suppliers, for example—although if you have an account and buy in volume, the price usually improves.

Working with Suppliers

Part of the suppliers service is to ask questions in order to clarify issues and confirm that your order is correct; they don't want to deal with a wrong order anymore than you do. When ordering allow time to carefully go over the order with the salesman to be sure it is correct. When the supplier sends an order confirmation or order acknowledgment, review again for errors.

The best salesman will tell you the truth, not what they think you want to hear. He will give you the best information available for products and services without embellishment or pressure to buy.

At some supply houses, you will find guys behind the counter with an attitude—plumbing suppliers are notorious—because you are not in that trade, they don't know you, or you are unsure of what you are asking for. Don't be deterred from asking for the information that you need and consider bringing your business to a friendlier place.

Some suppliers offer design assistance—ceramic tile, flooring, and kitchen-bath firms, for example—and they will work with you or your client to develop project designs and make product selections.

———————

Be wary of having a supplier do material take-offs. This has always been a questionable arrangement because take-offs vary so widely. For some suppliers, there is incentive to make the order as large as possible, while others will short the list, win the order on low price, and when the short is discovered charge for those items that were left off. Further, supply houses cannot accept responsibility for errors in their take-offs because they cannot control how material is used on-site, and thus they do not have the same motivation to be accurate that you do. Doing your own take-off assures that each supplier prices an identical list, which allows for a meaningful price comparison and ensures that the correct materials will be ordered.

———————

Specialty suppliers will do accurate take-offs for pre-manufactured items such as trusses, steel beams, windows, or cabinets (see previous note). These items are manufactured for a single purpose and are less vulnerable to misuse. Because of this, these suppliers are generally responsible for making it right if there is a problem.

———————

Develop a job site procedure to check each delivery. Be certain that the material is correct, there is no damage, and the right number of items was delivered. With some products—bundled flooring, boxed items, or very large stacked deliveries—it is not always possible to make an accurate count or to check for damage until the supplies are used. Note this on the driver's paperwork, and if problems are found later, let the supply house know right away. Use a camera to document the issues.

———————

Lumber, plywood, and hardwood all have grading systems, which are used to designate quality and use. Many job specifications require a certain grade of wood products to be used. Ask your lumber company to explain the grading systems—generally the folks at the box stores know less than you do—and where to get more information on the subject. Learn enough to use the grades and to be certain that you are getting the right product for the right application.[62]

If your favorite supplier does not stock a product you use regularly, ask them to. Most will be glad to do so.

Buy national brands when it comes to technical items like windows or roofing supplies. It is safer because you can trust that they will be around to honor warranties.

Read the directions each time you buy a new tool, piece of equipment, or vehicle. They contain a lot of "boilerplate" gibberish, of course, but they also include nuggets of useful, and, in some cases, indispensable information. Following this habit will save money and a lot of aggravation over the course of your career.

Inferior manufacturers will not stand behind their product. This is true no matter what their guarantee claims. If you have a good relationship with a supplier, in some cases they will feel obligated to force the manufacturer to make good or they will do it for them.

---

62 One supply house I was told about scraped the grade stamp off of lumber and mixed those pieces in with higher-grade lumber and sold it to unsuspecting customers.

Most product failures happen because they were installed wrong. It is rarely because the product actually fails.[63] Product use is often so specific and new products come on the market so often that it must be both personal habit and company policy to study the instructions before beginning an installation—even when that product has been used before. Allow time in the estimate for getting familiar with a product and insist that employees read the directions. Attend product demonstrations, ask salesmen for an on-site demonstration,[64] or go to the product web site for tutorials.

> "Why is it that there is never enough time to do it right, but there is always enough time to do it over?"
> —Anonymous

Be flexible and accommodating when suppliers make mistakes. Life throws curves at suppliers in the same way it does everyone else, therefore, if the overall organization makes an effort to be good at what they do, be understanding when the inevitable mistakes occur. If there are too many of them, try changing salesmen within the company, and if that does not work, change companies.

Pay your suppliers on time. A supplier is more likely to give you the best price if they know that you consistently pay your bills on time.

---

63 Of course, products do fail, and the supplier or manufacturer should make it right when they do.

64 If you are a good customer, the job is large enough, and the salesman knows the product, he may do this.

Restocking fees. If you made a mistake on a special-order item and it must be returned, know that a restocking fee is justified because it cost the supplier money to order it, and now they have to reverse the process and their supplier may charge them a restocking fee.[65] But some suppliers try to charge a restocking fee for in-stock items, claiming that they had to ship the item and then restock it when it is returned. Which is true. But it is also true that when their mistakes cost you money, you don't charge them. Therefore, in an ongoing relationship, it is a wash and there is no justification for a restocking fee on undamaged in-stock items.

———————

Call a supplier if you can't pay a bill on time. Whether it is because a customer is holding payment or some other mishap, explain the situation to the supplier and let them know when you expect to pay them. Chances are they will work with you for a month or so. But know that it can't happen often or you will lose your ability to charge with them. And know also that the worst thing you can do is not to say anything, avoid the calls asking for payment, or lie and say that payment is imminent ("the check is in the mail") when it is not.

———————

65 Many special-order items are not returnable and say so on the invoice.

CUSTOMER, CLIENT, OWNER

One who pays for goods or services.

A client, consumer, shopper, patron, buyer.

A person requiring professional services.

Clients should base their choice of a contractor on skill, service, experience, references, and then on price, but many don't. If clients try to force their big dream into a too-small budget, if on principle they don't believe that things should cost as much as they do, if they are only willing to proceed with the work if they get a bargain, or if they hire based on the lowest price, in the end they will go through a painful process and the end result will be an inferior product. Many will then loudly blame the contractor—and the building profession— rather than the criteria they used to select the builder.

In residential construction—barring theft, gouging, or incompetence—things cost what they cost within a fairly narrow range and what clients get with a misguided selection process and a too-small budget is a diminished product; this is a law, not open to exception. A diminished product means all or a combination of the following: poor planning; less skilled craftsmen; sloppy work; cheaper materials; late start and finish dates; illegal or questionable actions to avoid oversight; tension and frustration; a dirty job site; bad documentation; and poor financial controls. Because the construction process is complex and open to interpretation and variation, a "deal" is the very last thing a client should look for. Although you can't change this tendency, you can create a professional organization, charge what it costs to produce a quality product, and find customers whose main concern is professionalism, not price.

The right customers appreciate what you do; they are involved and interested in the project; they are willing and able to pay fairly and promptly; they understand the need for preconstruction planning and documentation; they stick with their decisions or are willing to pay for changes; they have a reasonable time frame; they expect you to make a profit; they understand that there are going to be difficulties and are willing to work through them without recrimination or retribution.[66]

Bad customers, regardless of how well you do your job, won't be happy. They nit-pick and complain; they don't pay their bills; they manipulate and deceive; they blame; they don't trust anyone; they are anxious and fearful; they are disappointed or angry most of the time; they can't make decisions; they are unreasonable; and many are emotionally unstable.

Shape your company around finding, selling to, and providing service in such a way that you attract the good ones, and the bad ones, if not weeded out in the sales process, find such clear organization—skilled staff, thorough contracts, excellent job documentation—that it is hard for them not to stay with the program. Get all of the components right—staff, product, price—and declining work from the bad clients will be easier.[67]

"A satisfied customer is the best
business strategy of all."
—Michael LeBoeuf

---

66 See *Fast Company* magazine "Innovation's No-Duh, No-Joke Secret Sauce: Friendship," Dec 9, 2011. See also *The Journal of Light Construction,* "The Nice-Customer Niche," Paul Eldrenkamp, Dec 2001, an excellent article and exactly right on every count.

67 The need to pick and choose customers depends on the service provided; well-defined jobs—replacing a toilet, changing out an A/C system for example—require less focus on the type of customer than more complex jobs. But regardless of the service, clear details and organization will make it harder for a difficult customer to ruin a good job.

CUSTOMER NOTES

Getting Work

Pre-qualify potential clients on the phone before meeting them face-to-face.[68] Some people are fishing for ideas and information; some already have a builder and want to check their price; some are going to do the work themselves but are curious how much it would cost to hire a builder; some are too hard to work with; and some can't afford to do the work they have in mind. It is pointless to meet people if there is no chance of getting work or if it is the wrong type of work.

———————

If you are meeting lots of potential clients but getting few jobs, improve your phone qualification process.

———————

If you are invited to bid a project, clients should be accessible: to take calls and return them, answer questions, and supply required information. If they aren't available or you feel they are annoyed or reluctant to give answers, they are almost certainly fishing for prices, not going to do the work at all, or not interested in you doing it.

———————

Church committees are usually difficult to work with. Talk with experienced contractors to understand what you are likely to encounter during planning, bidding, and on the job. Generally, you will find the level of sluggishness and confusion to be unmatched by any other organization. Take this into account in your pricing, negotiations, and schedule.

———————

68 See appendix for a sample list of questions: Prequalifying Client Phone Interview and In-Person Client Interview. Also see HomeTech Publishing website, under "Articles" see "Selling."

Be forthright and openly discuss everything that relates to the job. Some builders—both new and seasoned—will avoid telling customers anything they believe will upset them; this is poor customer relations and bad policy. The good customers will appreciate honesty and through the sales process a mutual trust and respect will develop based on it.

> "I give potential clients both good news and bad news, and I share uncomfortable opinions with them when necessary." —Dennis Dixon

When clients are certain what they want, suggest alternatives. As a young builder, when I met new clients who claimed to know exactly what they wanted, I tried to give it to them without elaboration. One of two things happened: I would lose the job to someone who improved on their idea or I would get the job and later they would ask me why I had not given them alternatives. In time, instead of being intimidated by their certainty, I found that asking questions about their plans softened most people's position enough to allow discussion and expansion. If clients will not budge, detail this in the contract, making it clear the clients insisted on the work being done their way.

Certain clients might require extra care. Often young couples or those who have no experience with building will at first seem difficult to work with because their inexperience makes them overly cautious. If they meet that all-important criterion of being honest and reasonable and you can add a little extra money for the handholding, it might be a good job despite first appearances.

When contracting to build a project with a group, require that one person be designated as the group's representative. This person will be responsible for relaying decisions to you and keeping the group informed. This will clarify communication, one person will be responsible for directions, and it will make the process run more smoothly. For your part, take direction from and discuss the project only with that person. If another group member insists on getting involved, ask the representative to rein them in.[69]

Lawyers and doctors are often harder to work for than the average client. It may be because they are highly educated or because they are used to negotiating. Whatever the reason, at one point in my career I stopped taking them as clients because every time I did I had problems: they did not pay their bills, they renegotiated every point, they threatened legal action to intimidate, or they took obvious contractual meanings and twisted them to get their way. I was young and my business was not as orderly or my contracts as complete as they should have been. So I'm not suggesting that you don't work for them, only that your contracts and specifications be doubly precise when you do.

---

69 On one job that had two partners, I was required to demolish a flat roof on a townhouse and replace it with a steep roof. During estimating, one of the partners told me that they were going to gut the house and I did not need to price in rain protection. When the rains came the second partner told me to protect the interior of the house. I spent a great deal of money that was not in the estimate tenting the roof and I could not increase the price because the first partner denied that he had said not to include rain protection.

Don't give ballpark figures no matter how much the person requests, demands, cajoles, or claims they understand it is a rough figure. It is a trick, an ambush, a ruse. Regardless of how many times you say, "this is a ballpark figure," when you give a number they are going to compare it with your actual estimate and draw unfavorable conclusions. Further, if you give a figure and someone else gives a much lower or higher one, you become suspect despite the fact it was a guess. They will, in spite of their claims, survive the wait.

––––––––––––

Do not give low numbers to avoid scaring clients. When first meeting with a potential client, young builders often estimate low numbers for the likely cost of the project because they are concerned the actual cost will scare the client away. But low-balling a price and then having to adjust the figure upward as the project begins makes you look either poorly informed or dishonest.

> "The most important persuasion tool you have in your entire arsenal is integrity." —Zig Ziglar

––––––––––––

Be careful when taking a job that another contractor has left. Talk with the people involved and look beyond your first impression. There are situations in which a contractor is incompetent or dishonest. There are also situations in which good contractors leave because of bad customers. If you determine that the customer is difficult, don't talk yourself into taking the work because it will be different with you; it won't be. Walk away.

––––––––––––

Be especially careful when a customer has started a project, run into trouble, and wants you to complete it. Clients sometimes begin a job—from measuring to designing to subcontracting to doing physical labor—but can't complete it, so they call a tradesman or GC for help. The potential problems are nearly without limit, and unless it is handled well, the outcome is likely to be a disaster. Appraise the current situation: Are there drawings and specifications and how good are they? What materials are ordered? Are the materials onsite correct and in good condition? What is the overall quality of the work? Is there weather damage? Are there things that need to be torn out? What agreements have been made or contracts signed with subs and suppliers? Are there permits? Have there been inspections? How much of the budget has been spent and what remains? If you decide to take the job after your appraisal, do it on a cost-plus or T&M contract,[70] charging for all of your time at your full rate. Carefully document the "as is" conditions, list all questionable issues, keep detailed records, and make the contract language sweeping in order to cover yourself.[71] Do not allow the clients' concern with cost to affect what you know needs to be done; if you cut corners, their initial mistakes become your problem. If they are unwilling do what is required, walk away.

---

70 It is nearly impossible to do an accurate estimate on a job in progress and utterly impossible when started by a nonprofessional.

71 Use a lawyer with construction experience to review the contract.

Do not give away your preconstruction products to potential customers. This includes estimate line item details, specifications, material take-offs, lists of your subs and suppliers, schedules, and ideas. Some people are educating themselves at your expense and will use as much of your time and all of the information you give them without ever using you. Design your sales process so that clients sign a contract before receiving this information.[72]

Include a time frame in every contract by which a client must accept your proposal or the price may be adjusted or the work turned down. Usually from 5 to 30 days. When you sign a contract there are legal obligations to do the work under the terms of the proposal. But proposals are developed around time specific conditions—weather, material costs, workload, subs availability—and if clients wait to accept a contract these conditions change. Also, if several outstanding proposals are accepted at the same time it may overwhelm the company. Therefore you must have a legal way to adjust the cost or decline the work.

---

72 A friend tells of a time he designed and drew an addition for a potential client, only finding out that he would not get the work as he drove by the home and saw the addition being built using the plans and specs he had provided for free.

Pricing

Avoid customers who try to squeeze lower prices or additional work out of you. If you give in to such demands to win the job, you will start in a hole, you will resent having done it, and they will continue this behavior throughout the project. Builders often believe that there is more free money in a project than there actually is and they may give some of it back to get the work, effectively buying the job. This is a downward spiral from which it is impossible to come away whole.

Allow money in your estimate for one or two return trips—depending on the size of the job—some months after a job is complete to touch up items as a gesture of good will and to strengthen your most important marketing tool: referrals from satisfied customers.

> "The first step in exceeding your customer's
> expectations is to know those expectations."
> —Roy H. Williams

Although the percentage you charge for profit may allow for a bit of negotiation, *give up every cent grudgingly.* A business cannot thrive and grow without robust profit.

Do not hide overhead charges from clients. Many contractors hide the figure in their bid to avoid discussing it, but at some point during the project there will be an issue that requires these charges to be disclosed and, not having been informed before-hand, many clients will resent the charge and some will refuse to pay it. Therefore, show your overhead and discuss it openly.[73] If clients are unwilling to pay it, you will know in advance.

---

73 This note refers to large jobs. On small projects overhead and profit should not be broken out. Some builders will disagree with this advice for any sized job. Research the idea and decide for yourself.

Charge for job planning and construction documents. Some clients see no reason to pay for job planning, claiming they know what they want and a professional should know what is required,[74] or that these costs should be in the price of the work because it will take only a "little planning." This is nonsense intended to persuade you to make the cost go away. Unfortunately some builders respond by skimping on planning or paying for it, either cheating the client or themselves. Regardless of the size of the job, the only way to give customers what they want is to understand their ideas and requirements and to work through the possibilities, make choices, and develop construction documents as dictated by the project's size and complexity.[75] Further, these costs will be paid one way or another, if not in the planning stage, than in lower quality, higher cost, and intense frustration as the details are worked out in wood and concrete. No matter how good you are, no matter how hard you work, nothing will make up for an unplanned job.

"Well planned is half built." —Anonymous

Some clients will claim that your overhead figures are too high and suggest a lower number—but if it is an accurate figure derived from the company's accounting, it cannot be reduced. It is as much of an expense as a box of nails, and it will be paid either by the client or the business.[76]

---

74 In fact the opposite is true; the more one knows, the more planning is done before starting a project.

75 The need for planning holds true for small projects, but because the planning required is limited the cost can be included in the bid. For example: a small deck built on the ground with no railings or steps needs limited planning and few documents while a raised multisided deck with railings, steps, plumbing, electrical, and specialty materials needs design and thorough documentation. Replacing a faucet needs a simple contract with a few details while the plumbing for a new house needs to be laid out, specified, and drawn. The cost for planning must be borne by the client, not the builder

76 This statement assumes a well-managed company; if overhead is bloated from poor management, debt, or extravagance that is a different issue.

Homeowner associations can affect a job. If you are planning to work in a subdivision with a Homeowners Association, realize that they often have legal powers—similar to building and zoning agencies—granted to them by their bi-laws, allowing them to mandate building setbacks and size and design restrictions among other things. Many of these organizations go dormant after a number of years and they exercise little or no control, while others, especially in high-end subdivisions, can be more restrictive and demanding than government agencies. Determine in advance how active they are and what they will require.

Some companies submit low bids planning to make up the shortage with change orders. That is, they try to win the bid based on low price with the idea of creating a stream of inflated change orders for every possible item. The less comprehensive the job documents the better for their purposes. For the client who has selected this company, it is going to be a long, contentious, and painful process.

Clients may ask that you lower the price on a product if they find the item for less. For example, if you priced ceramic tile at six dollars per square foot for material and they find the same tile for four dollars per square foot, they may ask that you credit them the difference. Don't do it, because on a competitively bid job, items that were priced high help to offset those that were priced low.

Job Preparation

Explain to customers at the pre-construction meeting how to handle problems. Explain that if they bring up problems early, before they are upset, they can be solved quickly. Some folks don't know how to say that they have a problem until it has reached crisis proportions. With these customers, make an extra effort to listen closely and ask questions to bring problems into the open. Once a problem is identified it becomes the company's responsibility to solve it quickly.

> "It is so much easier to be nice, to be respectful, to put yourself in your customers' shoes and try to understand how you might help them before they ask for help, than it is to try to mend a broken customer relationship." —Mark Cuban

Try setting up extra meetings with difficult customers. You might include them in job planning or other meetings with the hope that this will allow you more room to work. With some it will help, others will become even more difficult when provided with more information. Rely on the contract and job documents, use change orders liberally, and, if necessary, push back firmly to limit their interference.

Read *The Well-Built House* by Jim Locke and *House* by Tracy Kidder. Both books are an easy read and contain useful information about the building process. If appropriate, ask your clients to read all or at least key sections of each book which you believe will help them to understand the building process.

There are clients who believe they can benefit from the confusion of poor job planning. They reason that the builder will miss something on the bid and that they can hold them to the cost or they will be able to take advantage of the confusion by making subs eat cost overruns. But these situations cause intense resentment and folks working on the job will repay the deceit with lower quality, jacking up other prices, or out-right theft or vandalism.

Meet with all decision-makers during the planning stage of larger jobs. In the first few meetings you get to know each other and, as a group, discuss, define, and clarify expectations. If a decision-maker is not involved at this stage, it is nearly certain that they will become involved later, often when they are upset. Some customers, despite your explanation, will insist on one member being at the meetings and making all the decisions. It can work. However there will be a presence, unseen but felt, which you cannot affect and that complicates the customer-builder relationship. It is not unreasonable to decline a job because one or more of the clients is distracted, disinterested, or hostile toward the project. If you decide to take a job like this, talk with your lawyer and revise the contract to address these circumstances; there are legal issues when one party makes choices that bind a second party.

Run all special order items by the owner/designer before ordering. Have them sign a purchase order that includes all details confirming the choice: color, model number, price, and so on. Do this even when you feel certain what the choice is, because if the item is wrong—and even sometimes when it is right but they have decided they don't like the choice—you are responsible for making it right.

In contracts for larger jobs require that clients name your company as "an additional insured" on their homeowners insurance policy. This should cover completed work and building materials stored on-site and it should continue in force until the work is complete and paid in full. If the homeowner is unwilling to do this, carry a "builder's risk" policy and charge them for it. Ask your insurance agent for details.

––––––––––––

On larger jobs check clients' credit to confirm they can pay for the work. Check to see if they pay their bills and if they have the money to pay for the work they want done. With the customers' permission and for a price, credit agencies will provide a comprehensive credit report.[77] If clients are taking out a construction loan, ask to see the loan approval, or if they are paying cash, ask to see a bank statement showing they have the cash available. Ask your accountant for help understanding their financial information. Incorporate the request into your standard procedures and most people will provide the information willingly. If they resist, it could be that they are reluctant to expose their finances or it could be that they don't have the money required to do the work.

––––––––––––

---

77 The three largest U.S. companies are Equifax, Experian, and TransUnion (2013).

Suggest that customers move out when working on large sections of their home. Many customers will choose not to because of the added cost and inconvenience. But having them in the house during construction—and this is doubly true if there are kids and pets—is going to be more difficult for everyone. For the client, their daily routine will be disrupted, they will have little privacy, they won't be able to find what they are looking for, the house will be dirty, items will be damaged, the noise will be unbearable at times, and there will be a rotating cast of characters climbing all over their home. Builders and subs will have to take extra care to reduce noise, contain dust and dirt, and perhaps clean up language. There will be extra time spent working around, cleaning, and moving personal belongings. Some of your time will be spent soothing frustrated clients—"That is the third time I have asked them not to smoke in my home," or "I was using the toilet and he walked right in on me!"—and extra work will be required to satisfy clients' needs. If they are not going to move out, add money to the estimate to cover extra cleaning, barrier protection, downtime for accommodating the family, and having to work around a toilet or stove that has to be left in place temporarily. Let subs know before they bid that the family will be living in the home.

Do an on-site walk-through with the client and the major subs before each trades' rough-in begins. This allows clients to choose the location of items that are somewhat flexible such as switches, lights, and various outlets. Although approximate placement may be indicated on the blueprints, standing in the building will offer a better perspective to choose their locations. The sub will explain the options and mark the surfaces to indicate final locations. You or the foreman should be on each walk-through taking notes, discussing options, and guiding the process.

Be wary when clients want you to use a relative or "their" tradesman. They are trying to do someone a favor or save money. It is not always unreasonable and might work if your company is small and the client is willing to accept the inefficiencies inherent in this arrangement. But as a company grows, it becomes too disruptive. If the client pays the sub—as they generally will—who does the sub answer to? How can you affect their work? What if they second-guess decisions? If they won't listen, will you be forced to go to the owner for a decision, and, if so, who is running the job and who is responsible for its outcome? Explain the issues to the clients, they might understand and let it pass. Some clients will insist that you use their personnel, and, if you want the work, you might agree to it. But meet the person and interview them, check their work, make it clear in the contract that they take direction from you, require that they start on a trial basis and that you may end their employment if using them causes problems. If the client proposes using two or three of their own people, pass on the job.

If a client wants to work physically on their project, consider it. They may be interested in learning, or they want to save money, or they enjoy working with their hands. It can work if you are confident in what you do, you still work in the field, and they are easy to get along with. As the company grows, I think you will find it too disruptive to have owners working on their own projects.

On the Job

Record and file product information for each job you do. It should include general notes, where a product was purchased, cost, cut sheets, samples, and specs. The information will be useful when something needs to be repaired or replaced or when more work is requested. On larger jobs give the client a well-organized folder containing product information for their records, and file a duplicate copy with the job records.

———————

Leave small amounts of each item used on a job for the client. This might include a bundle of shingles, a roll of wallpaper, a few pieces of siding, a can of paint, or a box of floor tiles, for example. If clients need to patch or replace damaged material, they will have an exact match, and in the future if they add or redo something, they will have a sample and the product information to make the best possible match. Leave the items in a cool dry location.

> "Do your homework. The owners will treat your
>   opinions, directions and recommendations as gospel.
>   Choose your words carefully, communicate facts,
>   and if you don't know, say so!" —Dennis Dixon

———————

When working inside a home, make the customer responsible for safeguarding their valuables. Mention it in the contract and discuss it at the preconstruction meeting. Explain that, although you trust your employees, there will be visitors that you don't know such as delivery drivers, suppliers, neighbors, and building inspectors.

———————

Document jobs. Job documentation includes dated photographs or videos taken periodically over the course of the work, signed change orders, initials on blueprint changes, copies of correspondence, job-related paperwork, and a daily job log kept by the foreman recording phone conversations, meetings, when people and supplies arrived, which subcontractors were on-site, details of problems and their solutions, and other relevant and seemingly irrelevant facts. Create a clear job documentation procedure and follow it every day on every job. Allow for it in the estimate and schedule, keep up your end of it, and train your employees to keep up their end. File the information away when the job is complete. This information will be invaluable when planning other jobs, in negotiations, and when disputes arise.

———————

Clients' must be treated with respect by everyone in the organization. They will be easier to work with and more forgiving when problems arise.

> …patients don't file lawsuits because they've been harmed by shoddy medical care…it's how they were treated, on a personal level… [78]

———————

With particularly demanding customers it can be hard to know how far to go. You want to keep them happy, but some people have no sense of fairness and will continue to demand more as long as you give it. Discuss the issues with other builders to determine what is reasonable, and use the contract and construction standards as a guide to set limits and to push back when required.

———————

78 From the book *Blink*, by Malcolm Gladwell, "Listening to Doctors," pages 39-43. Read at least this section of the book because it explains the importance of a warm and respectful relationship between a client and their service provider.

Do not manipulate information to support your idea of how things should be done or to cover mistakes. You are often the only one to know all the facts on a job, so it can be tempting to spin them to your advantage. Don't. Lay out the facts as they are without manipulation or justification. If there has been a mistake, take responsibility as required. No one is perfect and things do not go right all the time no matter how skilled we are or how hard we try. To be clear and direct is not, however, to be rude or unconcerned.

> "If you tell the truth you don't have to remember anything." —Mark Twain

———————

You cannot be endlessly accommodating when running a job. You must allow for change—construction requires flexibility—but it is a process of building one item on top of the preceding one, both figuratively in the planning and literally during construction. If clients change their minds as if they were rearranging furniture, you have to get them to stop. Using change orders and charging for every expense—time delay, moving on and off site, rescheduling, re-planning, re-designing, re-permitting, demolition, all discussions, phone calls, research, and errands—will generally bring them to their senses.

———————

Remain honest and fair regardless of how difficult the circumstance or the customer become. This does not mean telling a difficult customer what you are doing to protect your company from them, but it does mean continuing to provide the service for which you were hired, giving clear answers, and discussing job issues as you see them.

> "Without courage, all other virtues lose their meaning." —Winston Churchill

———————

When problems arise on a job, young builders often give away too much in an attempt to be fair to the client. The best resolutions are fair to both the client and the company.

––––––––––

Don't get emotional when disputes arise. Negotiating with clients to resolve disputes should be viewed as a business transaction and given as little emotional charge as possible. If the client is emotional, listen and do not engage in defensiveness or blame. Gather the facts, understand the alternatives, and make the best decision the situation allows. And know that choosing to compromise in order to settle a dispute is not losing or failing; it is a business transaction and not personal unless you make it so.

> "To listen well is as powerful a means of
> communication and influence as to talk well."
> —John Marshall

––––––––––

If you have made several honest attempts to understand a customers' issues without success, you can be fairly sure they have a hidden agenda. They could be angry about something done or not done, or feel they did not get something that was due them, or they could simply resent the high cost of construction. Make every reasonable effort to bring whatever it is into the open and resolve it—and increase the ongoing job documentation.

––––––––––

Avoid "right or wrong" distinctions when disputes arise. A time will come, even with the best customers and your best effort, when there is a disagreement to which there seems to be no resolution. In these situations young builders tend to be angry and refuse to budge because they "know" they are right.[79] But with good customers, it is only a matter of right and wrong if you make it so. Instead the question should be how to resolve each issue practically and fairly. "Seek first to understand, then to be understood."[80] Try to work toward the central problem—keeping in mind that many issues have different but equally valid interpretations—and then attempt to work out a fair solution. Be generous—but fair to the company—being guided by common sense, the contract, and industry standards.[81]

> "In conflict, be fair and generous."
> —Tao Te Ch'ing

––––––––––

Do not allow payments to be put off until the end of the job. It is to the difficult customer's advantage to put payments off until the job is complete because at that point the builder has little power except to call, send bills, or file suit. Therefore, unless absolutely unavoidable, address every issue as it arises and allow nothing to be put off until all of the work is done.

––––––––––

Publicly acknowledge excellent work. Whether it's an employee, supplier, subcontractor, or designer, tell that person, the client, and other people on the job if appropriate. Consider earnest praise and recognition for work well done an important part of everyone's compensation and give it freely.

––––––––––

79 Never blame or threaten; rude or angry behavior—regardless of how certain you are of your point of view—will hurt your negotiating position and the long-term relationship with the client.

80 Habit 5 from *The 7 Habits of Highly Effective People*, by Stephen Covey.

81 See the bibliography for a partial list of groups that write industry standards.

The contract and job documentation are your best defense if a client becomes difficult, combative, or dishonest. Refer to them often in your discussions and increase your efforts to document issues that arise, including every demand that they make and each effort to satisfy those demands. Have clients sign for every item that is changed whether there is a cost involved or not and do not back off of the documentation if they appear to become more reasonable—it could be temporary or even a ruse to get what they want. Collect money exactly as the contract spells it out, and if they are not paying per the contract, pull off the job until they do.[82] And do not take on extra work for them unless it is an absolutely unavoidable part of the current contract.

———————

Do not put off completing the final punch list. For some contractors, this is the hardest part of the entire job. But dragging the job out eats up profit and tests the good will of the client, and punch lists have a maddening way of growing each time you return as the client adds "just a few more things." Get in, complete everything, and get out and *never, ever, EVER* make the customer hound you to finish the work.

> "[my father]… gave me his four-step formula for success: Get in, get it done, get it done right, and get out. It works." —Donald Trump

———————

---

82 Tread carefully. Be certain the work is completed per the contract and that the money is owed. Give the owner documented written warnings and a short but reasonable amount of time to respond before pulling off the job. Consider talking with your attorney before acting.

Do not publicly blame employees, subcontractors, or others for problems on a job. Blaming others is amateurish and it will seriously hurt morale, relationships, and the client's confidence in you. As the manager you are responsible for problems. This is not to say you should cover up mistakes, dishonesty, or incompetence; expect those responsible to correct the problem when appropriate. However, assign responsibility privately and never attempt to use another's actions to shift responsibility away from your company.

———————

PLANNING/ZONING, CODES/ INSPECTIONS

Planning & zoning [83] divides a municipality's land into sections—industrial, commercial, or residential, each with subsections—and provides laws and regulations governing how that land may be used. Planning and zoning departments provide zoning analysis, reviews, variances, and approval of permits. Zoning inspectors enforce zoning regulations.

Building codes are the laws and regulations governing the design, construction, repair, and alteration of buildings and related items, and they provide minimum standards of safety for life, health, public welfare, and property.

Model codes are created and maintained by an organization, the International Code Council (ICC) for example, that is separate from the state or municipality that enacts the building code. A model code may be "adopted as written" or "adopted with modification."

Codes are either prescriptive or performance based. A prescriptive code details how the work is to be done or which materials must be used. A performance-based code states the level of performance required but leaves the method to arrive at the result up to the designer.

Building departments oversee construction projects within a municipality: village, town, city, or county. Their task is to answer questions about construction,

83 Visit http://alexandriava.gov/uploadedFiles/planning/info/general_ design_principles.pdf, to see Alexandria, Virginia's *Design Principles* presentation. It is a clear explanation of the principles of planning and zoning. Also, look around Alexandria's website, http://alexandriava. gov/, to understand how one municipality organizes its departments.

inspections, permits, and related topics; to provide plan review and require changes as needed; to issue building permits; and to provide field inspections to determine code compliance. They issue an occupancy permit—which is the wrap-up of the zoning/coding/permitting process—by which the municipal authorities acknowledge that all requirements have been satisfied and that the building may be used as intended.

- **Plan reviewers** evaluate submitted plans to see that they comply with the current codes and regulations and detail those items that must be brought into compliance before a permit will be issued.

- **Building inspectors** visit job sites and confirm that the construction is in compliance with the codes and the approved plans; they sign off on each phase of work for each covered trade, allowing the next phase to be done; and they give final approval when work is completed. In large population areas, there are one or more inspectors for each trade. In smaller areas, one or two inspectors might cover all of the trades or a municipality may use a private firm for inspections.[84]

Licenses are required for contractors and tradesmen in many areas of the country and some require applicants to pass a certification exam as the base requirement for licensing. State or local authorities administer licenses and typically charge one fee for the test and a separate

---

84 Building departments sometimes allow a contractor to hire a private engineering firm to review jobs. For example, if the item being inspected is beyond the building department's expertise or their inspection schedule is slowing the job down or there is a problem with an individual inspector, hiring an outside inspection firm might provide a workable alternative. You will be required to pay for its service, and the outside firm will need to be approved by and ultimately answer to the municipality. See IRC, R104.4

annual fee for the license. Many areas also require a general business license that is renewed annually.

In the United States there are no federally mandated residential building codes.[85] Instead, states adopt a statewide code, which is then administered by its municipalities. Some states require or allow municipalities to adopt and administer codes of their choosing.[86]

Virtually every zoning and building department is organizationally and procedurally different from its neighbor. Therefore, visit each department that you will work with to learn how they are organized, to understand what they require, and to meet the staff.

> **Planning/zoning**, ask: How does this office affects the type of work you do? What is the submittal process? How long does a typical zoning review take? [87] How long does a variance typically take? Collect and read any literature they provide and ask how best to learn about their process.

> **Building departments,** ask: Which codes they use? Which addenda? What does the submittal process involve? How many sets of plans do you need to submit? What is the inspection sequence? Who reviews drawings? Who inspects jobs? Are inspectors assigned

85 The Americans with Disabilities Act (ADA) is a federal law that covers a private home only if it contains a business, such as a doctor's office or a hair salon. Those portions of the residence used for the business are subject to ADA requirements.

86 See a list of International Code Council's codes adopted by states; http://www.iccsafe.org/gr/Documents/stateadoptions.pdf.

87 You are asking what the likely timeline for a zoning review, a variance determination, or the permitting process will be. But in fact no one can give you a definitive answer because it depends on how quickly and thoroughly you do what is required, how busy the staff is, and the specifics of the project. And going in, there is no guarantee that you will be allowed to do what you intend.

specific jobs or are they rotated through every active
job in the system? Are small projects handled differently
than large ones, and, if so, how? How long does it take
to go through the permitting process? If plans need to
be revised and resubmitted, what does that involve? Do
they offer building code classes? Ask questions until you
understand their process and what you need to do to
work within their system.

As of 2000, a new comprehensive collection of building
codes was available in the United States: the International
Code, or "I-codes," which are maintained by the International
Code Council (ICC).[88] The International Residential Code
(IRC)—the one relevant to this book—is a stand-alone
code, that is, it contains within it all requirements for the
construction of single-family projects and townhouses, except
when it occasionally directs the user to a different code. The
new residential code combined and extended three regional
building codes, which were phased out. Unless you work in
an area using one of the older codes or no code, the IRC is the
one to learn. ICC offers educational programs and technical
publications for the IRC codes as well as offering support for
the older codes.

Buy the code books you will work with and study their
organization and terminology. If possible, take classes and
attend seminars. Each time a code requires something of
you, study that section. Knowing the codes will improve your
projects; submittals will contain most of what is required,
estimates will include code-related costs, and there will be
fewer problems as construction proceeds.

In large population areas, zoning and building departments

88 ICC codes include (2012): building commercial, building residential,
fire, energy conservation, plumbing, private sewage disposal, mechanical,
fuel gas, wild land-urban interface, existing building, ICC performance,
property maintenance, zoning, green construction, and swimming pool and
spa. ICC does not have an electrical code, but they reference the National
Electrical Code (NEC).

are a maze of divisions, regulations, and personalities. Always be respectful, but not intimidated. If you don't understand something, ask until you do. In municipalities that are run well, working with these offices will become just another part of the entire building process. In those that are run badly, it may be up to the local builders to force them to improve. As you learn the procedures, you will know when to go along and when to push back.

> Never forget that you're a member of your
> own community. Don't do something
> that you wouldn't like to see done."
> —Keith Richman

PLANNING / ZONING NOTES

Miscellaneous

Zoning may or may not be involved in a given project. If you are to build an addition on an existing home and the building parameters—building height, side- and rear-yard setbacks—fall within what is permitted in the zoning laws, you should only need a cursory zoning review. If features of the project exceed what is allowed in the zoning rules, the building will have to be designed to fit within the restrictions, or an application for a variance submitted, requesting that the rules be modified for this project. The variance process is generally time consuming and the outcome is rarely assured.

Employees charged with enforcing zoning and building codes are *not* legally responsible for their mistakes. They are agents of the municipality in which they work and, unless gross misconduct or malice is involved, cannot be held legally accountable.[89]

For new builders the best building departments are good teaching organizations. To a certain extent, builders can draw them into this role by amicably but persistently asking for information and clear answers.

The responsibility for conforming plans to existing codes falls to the designer of that project. If an engineer is producing drawings, if you are designing a deck, if a plumber is laying out a house: each is responsible to meet the current codes.

---

89 See IRC, R104.8

You may find poorly run building departments. Some are badly run, and some officials are overwhelmed, poorly trained, burned-out, or corrupt. Knowing the codes will help, remaining civil yet persistent will help, and pushing back every so often might also help. Thoroughly document the issues. If you are a member of a building association, ask if they can help before seeking remedies yourself. Consider contacting the heads of the appropriate departments—but expect push back; after all they are the folks allowing the poor performance in the first place—the municipality's governing council, and state agencies. Consider writing letters to the newspaper and, if the issue is obstructing your business, consider legal action.

———————

Understand the politics of building departments. All building departments are small in the sense that if you harass or irritate an official, you may face adverse consequences such as delayed inspections, an uncommon number of problems discovered during inspections, or plans taking longer to be reviewed than normal. Don't be intimidated, but be polite and use common sense when dealing with building officials.

———————

Buy code books. Because the building codes are legally binding, there is an ongoing debate about whether one should have to pay to read them or if they should be available for free. As of this writing, the codes may be found online for free, but buy the code books anyway. They will be up-to-date, easier to study and markup, and easier to refer to. [90]

———————

90 I found several online sites that posted current building codes. Some were state websites and some were private. None were official sites—that is maintained by the code writing/issuing agencies—and it was impossible for me to tell if they were complete or if the posts contained the most current version and addendum.

Buy the *Code Check Series* of books. They offer condensed guides to the most commonly cited code violations encountered by building inspectors and contractors. Each edition of Code Check is based on specific sets of codes, and most include summaries of code changes and link them to the prior edition of the codes.

The permitting/inspection process should be a verification of a builder's knowledge, not a process of discovery and redesign.

Expect changes when submitting plans for a building permit. More often than not, some changes or additions will be required. Depending on the complexity of the project, the building department's policies, and how extensive the required revisions are, it may be possible to make simple changes at the counter of the building department and have them approved or, more likely, they will need to be formally revised and re-submitted.

After the plans are approved and a permit issued, carefully study the notes and comments left by the plan reviewer and ask questions well in advance of starting the work.

Change orders that modify code compliance after a permit has been issued must be approved by the building department. For some changes the inspector may be able to sign off on-site, but for larger changes you will be required to go back through the building departments review process. Typically they will expedite approval for projects under construction.

For large jobs, schedule an on-site preconstruction meeting with your inspector. Review the plans and the job site with them and get their ideas about what to watch out for and what they are most concerned with.

———————

Post the building permit on-site so that it can be seen from the street. Put it in a window or in a weatherproof box on a post. In some areas you can be fined for not posting the building permit. Also, mark the property's address in large clear numbers at the street so that the inspector and others can find the project.

———————

Because each building project is unique, codes cannot cover every situation. Therefore officials are given some authority to interpret and clarify issues that arise so long as they adhere to the intent of the code.[91] Because it is simpler and safer, many code officials interpret questionable situations so that—at least from the builders' point of view—the least innovative of available choices is mandated. If a builder is convinced his method is best, he must prove that it meets or exceeds code requirements.[92] Unfortunately this process is expensive and time consuming, thus few builders can afford to make their point.

———————

The best inspectors understand both the code and its purpose. Thus, they may allow variations in construction methods that still meet the intent of the code.[93] Officials who don't understand the intent will adhere rigidly to a literal and often personally biased interpretation, usually forcing the selection of the least creative of the available options.

———————

91 See IRC, R104.1
92 See IRC, R104.11 and R104.11.1
93 See IRC, R104.10 and R104.1

It is common for an inspector to be replaced during a project—either permanently or temporarily because of vacation, sickness, or departmental reorganization. It is also common for the new inspector to focus on different things than the previous one, even sometimes contradicting the first inspector's indication that you are fully compliant. Although you could dispute the new requirements, it is generally more efficient to simply do what is required and move on, viewing the experience as an exasperating glitch in an imperfect system. [94]

Do not call for an inspection before the work is ready to be inspected. In some areas, a fee is charged if an inspector has to return a second time because the item was not ready. If you have a relationship with an inspector, he may allow some leeway, but discuss it with him in advance and don't assume anything.

You or a senior employee should be on-site when a building inspector arrives. If made to stand around, inspectors may find things that could have gone unnoticed. Also, train field employees to cooperate with and answer direct questions from inspectors, but *never* to offer more than they are asked. Many shops tell their employees to refer every question, no matter how trivial, to the foreman.

---

94 We once had an engineer-stamped and county-approved set of roof trusses correctly set and ready to sheath when a newly minted inspector required that we install 2 × 4 blocks along the run of each truss: it was not remotely within code requirements. Over the phone the inspector's boss agreed that the requirement was wrong, but we faced an estimated one-week delay to reverse the decision. We blocked the trusses and moved on. We also demanded and got a different inspector.

If you choose to dispute a decision by a code official, refuse to do what they request and ask that they issue a summons for the violation, and then go through the process of disputing it. If you are planning on disputing a decision, be certain that you're working from the current code and addendum.

———————

Do not lie to or deceive a building inspector. If you do and you are found out, building officials will be hypervigilant when looking at your future projects. On the other hand, you are under no obligation to point out minor code infractions that the inspector misses.

———————

You cannot always rely on approved plans to be correct. Even when everything has been done as required by law, stamped by professionals, and signed off on by the authorities, the builder remains responsible for code violations and anomalies, regardless of when they are discovered in the building process.[95] Although uncommon, this is another exasperating glitch in the system, which must occasionally be tolerated.[96]

———————

95 Depending on the circumstances, it might be an engineer, designer, sub, or the client who is ultimately responsible for correcting or paying to have an issue corrected.

96 On a new house we had installed and landscaped a driveway with a culvert as designed by an engineer and in the location stipulated on the state highway department's approved plans. A week before the house was to be sold, the highway department informed us that we had to move the driveway.

PROFESSIONALS

A professional is anyone who consistently practices and produces good results in their chosen field. For our purposes, professionals are those people who earn a university degree: engineer, lawyer, designer, or CPA, for example.

Do not be lulled into complacency by someone's title, position, or resume. A small percentage of professionals are exceptional at what they do, the center tier adequate, and the bottom tier dreadful. Analyze them as you would an employee: define the need, understand the options, conduct interviews, and call references. Ask people you respect whom they recommend. But do not choose simply on a recommendation, no matter how good it is. Call references and search the internet for ratings. And do not base your choice primarily on the fee. With a genuinely accomplished individual, a higher fee will be mitigated by speed, thoroughness, and the quality of the end product.

When hiring a professional, if you are uncertain what you want or your directions are vague, the result could be disastrous.[97] Clarify the need, define the end product, try to negotiate a flat or a not-to-exceed fee—barring that, understand the likely cost—and decide case-by-case how important the project is. If the business can't afford it, revise the task or look for other options. And do not allow an action to begin without understanding the details of what is being done and giving considered approval; you are responsible legally, financially, and morally for the actions taken on your behalf.

97 A friend asked a lawyer to draw up a will for his family. He had in mind a two or three page document. He got back thirty-nine single- spaced pages, which the lawyer had written from scratch, and a bill that literally took his breath away.

PROFESSIONALS NOTES:

Use professionals as advisors and to solve specific problems in specialized areas. Setting up a computer or an accounting system or developing a safety program are good examples of areas where professionals can help develop and improve your business. They are generally far too expensive for day-to-day tasks.

———

Hire professionals that have the specific expertise you need. If you hire a lawyer, for example, who does not have the right experience, the advantage, the very logic behind hiring a professional is lost. If you can't find someone in your area with the required expertise, find someone who fits your other requirements—integrity, skill, intelligence—and work out an arrangement that does not include paying him to learn what he needs to know.

> "An expert is a person who has made all the
>   mistakes that can be made in a very narrow field."
> —Niels Bohr

———

Periodically review the cost and the product of each professional you use. Adjust the relationship as needed, and end those that do not provide clear value. Every year or two consider having another professional review and comment on the work provided. Know what others are charging for their services, and if you are happy with your advisor but feel you are paying too much, try to negotiate a reduced fee. But do not leave a good relationship to save a little money.

———

ACCOUNTING; BOOKKEEPER, ACCOUNTANT, CPA

Accounting is the process and system of organizing, maintaining, analyzing, and auditing the financial records of a company. It is the physical process of gathering, entering, and tracking financial information into an accounting system—paper or computer—and extracting from it information in the form of reports and statements that detail the financial position of the company and from which informed business decisions can be made.

> "[accounting]…is a blink of history reduced to numbers….the accounting product is, at best, a report card; at worst, a cause of woe.… (it) is a guide for financial modification:…how is performance compared to expectation; where can activity be modified to meet objectives?" —David Fields

Bookkeeper, a person whose primary job is data entry and general record-keeping and related financial tasks. A bookkeeper will typically not have a formal accounting education. In small construction companies, the owner or spouse often does the bookkeeping.

An accountant (sometimes called a "comptroller") has a formal accounting education and does bookkeeping and analyzes the financial data generated by the accounting system. An accountant understands the more complicated issues of finance—balance sheets, cash flow, projections—and how they can be used to help direct and manage the business.

Certified public accountant (CPA): A CPA is an accountant who has passed a series of exams administered by the American Institute of CPAs and is licensed by the states in which he works; all CPAs are accountants; not all accountants are CPAs. A CPA must participate in ongoing educational programs and follow rules of conduct and ethics. CPAs can legally advise on tax consequences, do all accounting functions, and legally certify that a company's financial statements are correct. CPAs may offer advice when you open a business, and once it is operating, they can advise on financial issues, explain the tax results from business decisions, and do year-end taxes.

An accurate accounting system and an honest, meticulous bookkeeper or accountant are fundamental to a company's long-term success. Before choosing your accounting software or bookkeeper, find a CPA with residential construction experience and get his advice.[98]

You don't need to become an accountant, but you do need to understand the principles behind accounting and how to use the information to manage your business. Ask your CPA to teach you what he can, to recommend specific reading, and take a few classes to learn the basics. Regardless of who does your books or how large the company becomes, never relinquish involvement in the company's finances.

---

98 This is not a matter of taking the first CPA you come across, but choosing one with relevant experience and a great reputation.

ACCOUNTING NOTES

Miscellaneous

During times of financial prosperity, prepare for adversity. Downturns are inevitable.

———————

Keep accounting services in-house if you can. There are companies that offer those services—from individual accounting components to the entire process—but there is significant benefit to having most, if not all, of your accounting done in-house. Our CPA of many years said that, among his clients, those who did in-house accounting were the most profitable because they learned what the numbers meant and how to use them to lower overhead and production costs. Further, you care more about the result than an outside company does and, therefore, the information will be more accurate and more useful.[99]

———————

Computer Programs and Systems

Take the time required to choose the best accounting program for your company. When buying your first system it is difficult to know what you will need, therefore do extensive research and use your CPA and bookkeepers knowledge and experience to help choose the best one for you. If you choose well you could end up using the same software for your entire career. The very last thing you want to do is to cross your fingers and hope you are getting the right one.

———————

99 Some services, notably payroll and profit sharing, may be farmed out because they are less critical to daily operations and a specialized firm may be better equipped to handle them.

You will find information about construction accounting and software systems in trade magazines and trade associations.

———————

Don't buy the biggest or most complex accounting system available. Some are so difficult to use that the effort far exceeds the benefit, and chances are that you will never use their full capacity anyway. Instead buy a proven system that can grow with the company. Unless you have clear and compelling reasons to go with software from a new company, choose an established one; the new company may go out of business and leave you stranded.

———————

Be wary of changing computer programs and systems. The latest systems seem innovative and promise the world, so it can be tempting to change the established ones for a newer version. But changing computer systems requires a herculean effort and great expense, and it will disrupt the entire organization. In the end, there is no perfect software. Therefore, before changing systems do extensive research to fully understand what is required and what it will cost and how much time it will take—whatever you estimate, double or triple the figure— and be absolutely certain that the advantages far outweigh the expense and disruption it will cause.[100]

———————

100 We changed our accounting system at least four times over the years. Each new system promised ease of use and clarity; none lived up to the promise. With hindsight, we would have been far better off if we had chosen one accounting program in the beginning and stuck with it.

Some accounting firms request or even require that you use the software they recommend. But your company will use the software daily while the CPA will use it only occasionally, and the recommended program may not be the best one for you. Use theirs only if it is not overly complex or expensive and it provides what you need. Discuss this issue before hiring an accounting firm.

CPAs, Accountants, Bookkeepers

Use your CPA as a source of education and counsel. Call with questions and expect a prompt response and useful answers. Spend an hour or so with your CPA every month until you understand accounting as it affects your business and then switch to quarterly or semi-annual meetings to review and discuss financial issues and solutions. Your goal is to become familiar with accounting principles and to use them to mange and improve the business.[101]

Excellent bookkeepers are intensely well organized. They are exact in method and procedure, and they will make the business significantly better. When hiring, call several references, ask your CPA to interview them, do a criminal background check, and interview them a few times before making the hire.

---

101 Read "Accounting Habits of Successful Contractors" by Stuart Lerman in *The Journal of Light Construction*, March 2002, for a discussion of the type of accountant that you need and other useful information.

Practices

Study your company books once a week for the rest of your building career. Spend time by yourself studying the books and making lists of questions about things you don't understand—about accounting in general and the company books specifically—and get answers to those questions.

Go over the company accounts every week or two with your bookkeeper. Ask questions, especially the hard ones. It must be clear where every dollar comes from and goes to. And the information must be accurate and accessible through reports and statements. Once the system is up and running, if you are not getting that, if the information always falls just short of answering all your questions, replace the bookkeeper.

Have the company's financial records audited by an outside party regularly. This should happen every year of so and any time you have concerns. Embezzlement is common in construction companies, which is one more reason you can never relinquish knowledge of and ultimate control of the accounting. A good rule of thumb: trust, but verify.

Pay those taxes that the law requires and no more. Choose an accountant who aggressively seeks legal tax shelters and avoids every tax that can be legally avoided, and not one who passively agrees to pay everything that you could possibly owe for your safety or their convenience.

> "Any one may so arrange his affairs that his taxes
> shall be as low as possible; he is not bound to choose
> that pattern which will best pay the Treasury…".
> —Judge L. Hand

An accurate bookkeeping system discourages theft. If a potential thief knows that someone is watching, they will be less likely to steal, and if they do steal, they will not get away with it for long.

Signing checks keeps your finger on the pulse of the business. Do not relinquish this task until the company has grown so large that it is unrealistic. And require that each check have documentation with it—invoices, notes, job records, purchase orders—about what is being paid, why, and to whom. There may be other people in the company who occasionally sign checks, but you should review every one.

Never give employees who are allowed to cut checks the authority to sign them.

Lock up the checks. Pay attention to check numbers; there should never be one that is unaccounted for or out of numerical sequence. [102]

Restrict the number of people who spend company money. Be certain that what is spent can be traced back to who spent it and on what. Review every charge weekly; it is remarkably easy to lose track of what is spent, by whom, and why.

---

102 We had checks stolen from the back of our checkbook and did not discover it until the checks cleared the bank.

FINANCIAL PLANNING / FINANCIAL ADVISOR

Financial planning, while accounting tracks the flow of money, financial planning manages money to produce the maximum growth and to meet specific goals, such as building financial reserves, eliminating debt, or saving for college and retirement.

Financial advisor (also called investment planner, financial planner, investment advisor, wealth manager, asset manager, investment counselor, or portfolio manager) analyzes your current finances and helps you develop goals and investment strategies to reach those goals.[103]

You are never too young, your business too small, or your assets too modest to learn about and use financial planning. The sooner you start the better. Financial advisors range from the individual working out of their home to multinational corporations. Choose an advisor with good references, a long track record, and reasonable fees. If anyone—a friend, your CPA, your father-in-law—recommends an advisor, do not be intimidated into using them. Ask for documentation and research the advisor online.[104] Many financial advisors break even or lose money for their clients and some do well for a time and then begin losing money. Whomever you choose, remain intimately aware of the finances they control for you.

---

103 Watch "The Retirement Gamble" on PBS's *Frontline,* by Martin Smith, April 23, 2013. See an article in *Consumer Reports* entitled: "Truths Financial Pros Won't Tell You" October 2013, page 14, and search *Consumer Reports* for related articles.

104 Check these websites to find out if there have been disciplinary actions against a financial advisor you are considering: cfp.net/search, finra.org/brokercheck, adviserinfo.sec.gov. Also see apps.finra.org/datadirectory/1/prodesignations.aspx for an explanation of nearly 100 financial designations.

Interview at least three advisors—the initial meeting(s) should be free—and ask each to explain their typical client, their methods, and their philosophy. What training have they had? How long have they been doing it? Are they full- or part-time? How much money do they manage? How many clients do they have? Are they forthright? Do they explain what they do in terms that you understand? Are they someone you want to work with? Call references. Discuss candidates with your CPA, but do not use your CPA as an investment advisor. Ask what the advisor expects of you. Understand their fee structure and how and when they are paid. If possible use someone whose charges are based on merit—on how well your investments do—not on a flat fee that they get regardless of performance. Meet a second or third time—again free—with the most promising ones to check your first impression and to ask those questions that have arisen since the first meeting. *Be skeptical of anyone who claims amazing financial prowess.*

"You gain strength, courage and confidence
by every experience in which you really
stop to look fear in the face."
—Eleanor Roosevelt

BANKERS/LENDERS

Commercial banks, credit unions, and finance companies are businesses, not community services. They don't loan money because they like you; they make loans to people they believe will pay their bills on time and in full. If a bank turns you down for a loan, don't blame them, work to improve your finances.

Like other businesses, lenders—banks, savings & loans, credit unions—fail. Check online for reports on the financial health of any financial institution that you are considering using.

Financial institutions are in the business of storing and lending money and they need good customers as much as you need a place to put your money.

Consider using a credit union instead a bank. They are focused on the local economy, and they tend to have fewer rules and better rates on savings and loans.[105]

Establish a friendly relationship with your financial institution. Introduce yourself to the account manager. Make a point of calling that person every so often to discuss your accounts and to better understand the services available to you. Consider taking them out to lunch once a year.

Consider taking out a loan when you don't need it. Put the money in a savings account and don't touch it. Pay it back according to the terms of the loan to establish a track record with the lender. Because loan information is shared with credit agencies, this will also help establish or improve your credit rating

Get "preapproved" for loans for big purchases. You will know in advance if you can get the loan and if the terms are acceptable and you won't spend time preparing for the purchase only to discover that you don't qualify. Also, when

---

105 See an article in *Consumer Reports* entitled: "CREDIT UNIONS: Now almost anyone can join," March 2007, page 47. It explains the advantages of using credit unions over other financial institutions.

you find what you are looking for, you will not lose it to someone who has cash in hand.

The Small Business Administration (SBA)[106] is one possible source for loans. SBA loans have several advantages over those from commercial lenders: lower rates, more favorable terms, and fewer restrictions on who qualifies. But the loan process is more complex and exacting. In the SBA program, a commercial lender makes the loan with the SBA guaranteeing a large portion of it. There are pros and cons to SBA loans, so learn what they are and how to go about getting a loan from the SBA well before you need it. Commercial lenders with experience making SBA loans will get approval faster and with fewer glitches than lenders with no SBA experience.

If your financials are strong, fees and loan rates will be lower. The weaker your finances the more you will pay to borrow money because you are a greater risk for defaulting on the loan.

"Most people struggle with life balance simply because they haven't paid the price to decide what is really important to them."
—Steven Covey

---

106 Visit the SBA website for information; http://www.sba.gov/.

CONSULTANT

A business or management consultant is anyone who advises a business for a fee. A lawyer or an engineer might be considered a consultant, but typically the term is reserved for an independent advisor who comes in for a limited time to solve a specific problem. Some are generalists, able to help with the overall organization on a broad range of issues, and some are specialists, working on personnel, finance, or computer issues, for example. Consultants are available in dozens of categories in every industry.

Consultants assist by using their knowledge and experience to evaluate that part of the organization that needs to be improved or extended and developing a plan to effect those changes. The plan may then be implemented by you, your staff, your staff with help from the consultant, or by the consultant alone. Consultants are used to avoid rookie mistakes when opening a new division; to bring objectivity to an intractable problem; to improve hiring; to coach or counsel employees and management either one time or on an ongoing basis; to expand the knowledge and skill of the owner; or to develop a particular project. Find consultants by asking business associates and by a search of the web.

The better you define what is needed—name the issue, outline a useful result, set a timeline and a budget—the more likely you are to find the right consultant and the more likely they are to succeed in helping you. But given that you don't yet fully understand what is required, your first efforts to define it are likely be clumsy and inaccurate. Do it anyway. Wrestling with the problem will make the solution easier to see, to implement, and to know when it succeeds.

It takes courage to open your business to an outsider. But with a good consultant, it is also one of the best ways to improve the company or solve a problem. Hire well, give your full attention to and do not resist the knowledge and new ideas that they offer.

> "Progress is impossible without change;
> and those who cannot change their
> minds cannot change anything."
> —George Bernard Shaw

CONSULTANT NOTES

Hiring Consultants

Think of consultants as white collar subs. Follow the same guidelines to hire and work with them—and to let them go.

———————

Although phone interviews with a consultant may work, they are less effective than working face to face.

———————

Consider creating a "request for proposal" (RFP). This is a formal process that requires upfront work by your company to develop the request, but it could provide more options. Look online to learn how to create an RFP. When it is complete, send it out to several consulting firms.

———————

Consultants typically charge an hourly rate plus expenses. But if the project parameters are clearly defined, it may be possible to do a fixed price or percentage contract.

———————

Ask consultants these questions: How long have they been doing this? Are they full-time? How many clients do they have? What projects have they recently completed? Were they successful? What is their educational background? How much specific experience do they have in what you need? How large is the organization and who will work on your project? Ask for samples of their work and ask them to talk about recent projects. Ask them how, if hired, they would proceed and what they would require of you and your staff? Discuss cost and billing.[107]

———————

107 Their resume and company literature will contain much of this information, but listening to their answers, you will get to know them and be better able to decide if they are the right fit.

Ask their references these questions: Did they stay on budget? Were there issues with billing? Did they solve the problem? Did they meet deadlines? Did they get along with staff? Did they analyze the problem correctly? Did their solution work? Were they accessible? What problems arose and how did they respond? What could they have done better? Did the person who was expected to do the work do it or did someone else step in? Was it worth the cost? Would they use them again?

———————

Consultants will be interviewing you to decide if you will be a good client. Not every potential client matches the consultants' requirements any more than every consultant's skills and abilities match your needs or budget.

———————

Be certain you are hiring the consultants' expertise, not providing on the job training. Their accumulated knowledge, experience, and education in the area you need help with is what makes their service valuable.

———————

Don't reject a consultant's proposal based on cost alone. He may be the best consultant with the best plan and well worth the money or he may be willing to negotiate his fee.

———————

Working with Consultants

Whoever you hire, insist on a well-defined process and unambiguous results.

———————

Give consultants the access they need. Be certain they get whatever company resources and information they need to do their job.

———————

Do not hand over your business to the consultant. No matter how skilled they are, they are not going to miraculously fix your problems. You and your staff must be closely involved in the process and in implementing the solutions.

———————

Maintain ultimate control. Discuss their progress regularly. If problems arise address them immediately and resolve them to your satisfaction or end the relationship. The contract must allow for immediate termination of their services without penalty.

———————

Consultants often find that the owner's limitations are a company's biggest problem. Before hiring, look honestly at yourself: Are you mature enough to face fears? Is your ego too large or too fragile to hear and act on criticism, to face hard truths, to make personal changes? If so, you are not ready to use a consultant.

> "He that won't be counseled can't be helped."
> —Benjamin Franklin

———————

Potential problems with consultants: providing management fads as solutions, developing plans too complex to implement or detailing a solution so loosely that it is meaningless, providing an unusable product, advocating a process with no end in sight, lack of specific experience or knowledge on which to base advice, repeatedly stating the obvious, providing banal instead of innovative solutions, providing solutions that don't fit the need, or billing for time not worked.

———————

DESIGNER

Designer, [108] one who studies to become certified or licensed to develop the designs and create the documents used to construct a project. Engineers sometimes develop residential construction documents and most permitting agencies accept an engineer's stamp in place of a designer's stamp.[109]

Design, to conceive, to imagine, to create in the mind what will be built.

Planning, making the design tangible by detailing the project in job documents, essentially prebuilding it by detailing the choices in drawings and specifications.

Design-build firm (DB),[110] a single company that performs both the design-planning and construction services. Variations on this model include a building company forming a partnership with a designer, either informally or legally, to offer their combined services, or a designer or builder subcontracting to the other in order to offer the full DB service.

Design-bid-build firm (DBB), one firm completes the design-planning process and, with completed documents, directs the bidding process, helps to choose and contract with the selected general contractor, and

108 I have used the term *designer* for everyone that creates job documents.

109 This is a partial list of organizations in the United States that train and certify or license designers: The Design-Build Institute of America (DBIA), The American Institute of Building Design (AIBD), The American Society of Interior Designers (ASID), The National Kitchen & Bath Association (NKBA), and The American Institute of Architects (AIA).

110 In *The Journal of Light Construction* see "Hiring An Architect," January 2003, and "dba Design-Build," June 2007, both by Paul Eldrenkamp. Also see "The Design/Build Process," J.J. Hayes, April 2007: on line at http://paradigmprojects.com/index.php/methods-of-work/the-designbuild-process/

then oversees the construction process. Variations on this model include different levels of service for each stage—design-bid-build—and different combinations of the three services.[111]

Design-planning happens on the smallest and the largest projects but many builders and tradesmen act as if it is something to be gotten through quickly in order to get to the "real work of construction." But this is a mistake. Good design benefits the client, the builder, and the community. Good planning assures that the result matches the clients' requirements and that the job runs smoothly. Companies providing and working with skillfully designed and planned products gain a significant competitive advantage. Who does the design-planning varies based on the clients' wishes, project size, region, trade tradition, and the planners' capability, but it breaks out very roughly as follows:

1. The majority of small to mid-sized residential projects are done through a collaboration of client and builder/tradesman or specialty firm. It is less formal than the design-build or design-bid-build process and the job documents consist of a contract, specifications (often included on the contract, but sometimes separate), and a few basic drawings. This may be anything from replacing a dishwasher, to painting, to upgrading an electrical panel, to a thousand other projects.

2. An addition or renovation requires multiple trades and detailed job documents and therefore a more extensive design-planning process becomes necessary.

3. For new homes there are several options.

    a. Pattern books or online plan sites offer hundreds

111 Toward the end of this section see Design-Build versus Design-Bid-Build for a detailed breakdown of this subject.

of stock blueprints and specifications at far less cost than a custom design. The downside is that too often owners can't find just the right plan to fit their needs, few include electrical, plumbing, or HVAC information, and in my experience these plans contain significant errors and meager specifications, thus requiring a great deal of work to make them usable.

b. Pre-fabricated (pre-fab) homes are built in a factory and delivered in various forms and in various states of completion. Their price tends to be lower, although not always. They offer limited floor plans and fewer options, and there is a perception of inferior quality—thus they are often restricted to the lower end of the market.[112]

c. Some companies pre-frame and ship wall, floor, and roof sections or sandwich panels developed from plans that you provide and which are then assembled on-site.

d. Companies that specialize in home building often have stock building plans available. They are not completely custom, but generally simple revisions may be made to more closely meet the clients' needs, although if the changes are extensive the cost may rival a custom design.

e. At the high end of the residential market, there are two methods for developing custom plans. The first is the design-bid-build model, the one promoted by many design firms, although significantly, not all. Many advocate for

112 In my career I have been aware of dozens of pre-fab companies that started—often with a new technology or material and some with a high-end product—but every one of them failed. Although the pre-fab business model offers the promise of high-quality standardized construction with cutting edge technology at lower overall cost, to my knowledge, it has only worked in fits-and-starts in the United States.

design-build. The second is the full-service design-build model which in many ways is the logical extension of the collaboration between client and builder mentioned in item one in this list.

When asking for clarification on a construction detail, builders will sometimes hear designers say with some exasperation, "that is a standard construction detail!" Often, not having provided enough detail, they are trying to let themselves off the hook. And while there are standard construction details, part of the designer's job—and for the builder, one of the most important ones—is to choose which details to use from the thousands available. On the other hand, no designer, regardless of skill or budget can get all of the client's desires or account for the variable nature of a construction project in the job documents. So, there is a balance, in which the best designers provide as many details as they can while the builder applies his common sense and willingness to work out noncritical details. But err on the side of caution because it is common for the builder to choose details only to be required to change them when the designer or the client does not like the choice.

DESIGNER NOTES

Principles

Good designers make a builder's life easier. They bring good esthetics, complete job documents, and ultimately greater customer satisfaction.

———————

Plan carefully if you want to evolve from a construction firm into a design-build firm. This may be a natural progression for many, but there are complex issues that need to be addressed. Research the subject thoroughly and develop a plan before beginning to head in that direction.

———————

For some commercial design firms, residential construction is what they do when work slows, claiming that it is simple compared to commercial work.[113] But this is roughly equivalent to a truck designer designing a one-off luxury car. It indicates the design firms' ignorance of the subject or just how badly they need work. The finer points of a home, the nuances that make it buildable, livable, and appealing are acquired through years of experience.

———————

New estimators need to ask lots of questions. But many are reluctant to do so for fear of exposing their ignorance. Get over this idea quickly and ask as many questions as necessary because this is one of the very best ways to learn.

———————

113 Commercial construction companies often do the same thing, frequently with the same poor result.

Bidding with Designers

Ways builders interact with designers:

- Be hired by a client and together choose the designer.

- Hire the designer as a sub or employee.

- Bring a client to the designer and be given the project.

- Be hired by a client at a designer's prompting.

- Subcontract to or be employed by the designer.

- Work with a designer in a partnership, either informally or legally.

- Be awarded a contract after a competitive bid managed by the designer.

Designers want to work with organizations, with people, with whom they have an amiable and professional relationship. Exactly as you do with employees, subs, and suppliers.

You will almost certainly need to submit bids to design firms when starting out. The bad news is that you will spend a great deal of time and resources with little to show for it. The good news is that you will refine your plan reading, estimating, and sales skills. For many builders, their long-term goal is not to bid competitively.[114]

---

114 See the Bidding section for more details.

Some builders work their entire career on jobs planned by design firms because it fits their temperament and their business goals. If this appeals to you find the best and the most collaborative design firms in your area, learn what they are looking for from their builders, and shape your company around providing it.[115]

———————

Many established builders bid only with designers with whom they have a collaborative relationship, whose work they know to be detailed enough to produce an accurate bid, and who ask for bids from no more than three qualified bidders. While others work only with designers they hire, either as a sub or an employee.

———————

Check with other builders before bidding with unfamiliar designers. Call two or three builders they have worked with to discuss the quality of their documents and how they interact on the job. In effect, you are calling their references. This may seem audacious but you cannot waste your time bidding with a designer who produces poor documents, avoids responsibility, or is impossible to get along with.

———————

Before bidding with a new firm, review one or two of its recent job documents. If the specifications and drawings are poor, pass on the work. Unfortunately, it is often difficult to tell how complete a set of drawings is until doing the estimate, and some flaws aren't apparent until the work is underway.

———————

115 A friend who was a builder in the San Francisco area worked for years with an architectural firm that produced complete job documents and worked to form collaborative relationships with the client and the builder on each project. Unfortunately I know far more builders for whom such a relationship, and such a design firm, was a fond dream.

If the plans you are bidding are so vague they require randomly padding the estimate to cover what is not detailed, you are wasting your time. Either do the estimate with a broad brush—an inflated square foot price, for example—or walk away entirely.

———

While doing an estimate, ask the designer for clarification as often as necessary. Cover yourself in the bid and contract by adding allowances, spelling out exceptions, and noting ambiguous issues.

———

The best design firms have a rigorous selection process for the builders they work with. They know that to get their projects built well—quality workmanship, as-designed, in a professional atmosphere—they must choose partners who are skilled, experienced, amiable, and excellent communicators.

———

When you are new or unknown to them, it will be difficult to get work from the best design firms. Make it easy for them: Do a couple of estimates even when they are checking prices. Find someone they know to recommend you. Send them a reference list and photos of your work. And walk the fine line between persistence and annoyance by reminding them in creative ways that you are available. When you are given a chance, do great work.

———

Be ready before you contact design firms. Every construction market has a limited number of good design firms. Do not contact the best ones until your business provides an excellent product and service. If you engage them too soon and disappoint, it's unlikely you will get a second chance. And when you are ready, contact them one at a time to be certain that you can handle any work that you get.

———

Before introducing a client to a design firm—assuming that you want the work and that you are qualified to do it—meet with the designer and agree that they will do all they can to ensure you get the work. If they say that you will be put on a list with other bidders, find another firm or sign the construction contract with the clients first and then hire a designer.

Design firms provide different services for clients—from site selection and acquisition to site plans, engineering, conceptual design, schematic drawings, detailed drawings, interior design, construction documents, managing the bid, selecting the contractor, negotiating the contract, administering construction, and final inspection—and various combinations of these services. What the client buys determines the amount of information provided in the job documents. Therefore, to better understand what is required of you, ask which services the design firm will and will not provide.

Stick with a good designer but do not become completely dependent on them. When you find a design firm that produces good plans and with whom you work well, try to work with them over and over again, but do not rely solely on one firm. If there is a falling out, if that firm closes its doors or shifts its focus, you will be in trouble.

Avoid designers who for budget reasons provide incomplete job documents. Some designers get involved in projects knowing there is not enough money to develop a complete set of job documents. They do as much as they feel they can afford to and put the incomplete product out to bid. The items they fail to provide will cause significant problems for the bidders, the builder, and the client.

Hiring Designers

When hiring designers, understand what you will and will not get. Are they providing a complete set of plans and, if so, what does and doesn't that include? How many pages, elevations, floor plans, sections, details, and of what items? Are they providing complete specs and what will and won't they include? What will you need to provide? Will the plans be sealed? Can you get a permit with the completed plans? Who owns the electronic drawings? If mistakes arise when building or submitting for a permit, will they correct those issues? Are printed plans and specs included and, if so, how many sets? Listen carefully while they answer your questions and explain their process and write everything down.

––––––––––

On the Job

The caliber of job documents varies greatly. You will find significant variations in the quality, quantity, and accuracy of the information provided from firm to firm and sometimes within the same firm. There are industry standards, but they are open to interpretation and opinion and affected by the designer's level of skill and professionalism, what the client is willing to pay for, and time constraints.

––––––––––

Study the job documents carefully and ask questions. If you don't catch a detail included in the plans, either big or small, you are responsible for correcting it if the item is built wrong.

––––––––––

When possible, work out mistakes and problems directly with the designer. Avoid pointing out their mistakes in front of the client.

––––––––––

When you find a detail in the job documents you believe could be done differently—better, faster, lower cost—discuss it with the designer or the client, but don't decide on your own or let a sub decide to ignore what is provided or you may be required to correct it at your expense.

———————

DESIGN-BUILD VERSUS DESIGN-BID-BUILD

Design-Build (DB): one company develops the job documents, estimates the work, and builds the project for the client.

Design-Bid-Build (DBB): a design firm develops the plans and the project is then put out to bid or the client negotiates with a builder to do the work.

Advantages of DB for the client

- The DB model places the responsibility for errors and omissions on the DB team, relieving the owner of much of the managerial responsibility and legal problems that so often arise when the functions are divided.

- Less paperwork and fewer construction details are required to be developed by the DB firm because the construction staff is involved in the design-planning process. Further, this familiarity means a faster and more informed start when construction begins.

- Because the field staff has a direct connection to the designer, once work begins, construction problems are solved in-house without needing to involve the client.

- The entire company's expertise and experience—including the foreman, estimators, tradesmen, suppliers, and subs—are available to help make the end product practical and cost effective.

- It is faster because parts of the construction process—schedules, budgets, lining up materials and subs, and the permitting process among others—can sometimes happen while the design-planning is taking place.

- In some cases, projects can be "fast-tracked," that is construction begun while the design-planning process is ongoing.[116]

- Warranty issues for design and construction rest in one place. Therefore, there can be no disputes about who is responsible.

- Having the project under contract, the construction department can focus their full attention on doing a detailed and accurate estimate.

- Hiring a builder based on reputation and skill is the surest way to develop an enthusiastic and productive team atmosphere.

- With the estimating department's help, the design is guided by the budget, making it far less likely that it will require redesign and rebid (see third point under Disadvantages of DBB for the builder).

---

116 Fast-tracking is done in DBB situations, too, but with a fixed-price contract, the builder is at a major disadvantage working in this way.

Disadvantages of DB for the client

- A company not exclusively focused on design may not provide the best option for a client interested in a specialized style or in a cutting-edge design.

- Because the same level of detail is often not required in DB as in DBB, the contractor may be in a position to claim that a lesser quality item or a less elaborate detail was included in the original bid figure.

- The client will be left without a second design professional overseeing the project, thus losing the possible benefit of another's viewpoint on complex or difficult issues.

- If a client feels that the only way to be certain that they are not paying too much is to get bids from several contractors, DB will not work for them.

Advantages of DBB for the client

- The DBB model incorporates competition into the process, allowing clients to feel that they are getting the best value available.

- Using the DBB model in a down market may allow the client to take advantage of lower prices from subs and suppliers.

- A firm specializing exclusively in design may be better at it than a company that has a split focus.

- Having the designer-architect oversee the building process may give the client a better quality product.

- The friction between the designer and the contractor may provide an atmosphere in which their complementary skills produce creative differences from which better solutions may be found.

- The client may be reassured by the vetting process used to select contractors.

Disadvantages of DBB for the client

- If the job documents are not thorough and accurate, there will be problems during construction, including significant time delays, cost overruns, and intense friction between the parties.

- If the clients' decision is based primarily on cost, the bidders must have nearly identical estimating and building experience as well as a similar workload and overhead, otherwise bids that come back are nearly meaningless and selecting a qualified contractor is a crapshoot.

- Design-Bid-Build is not a team sport; conflict is inevitable and the client will often be drawn into these conflicts. Lawsuits are common between parties.

- The DBB process generally costs more, often significantly more, than the DB process.

- It takes longer for the DBB process, often months longer.

- A line item bid is the most accurate type but when providing free bids, most builders use a quicker, less accurate method. This makes the final figures suspect and, because the job documents have not been gone through carefully, problems often go undiscovered, thus assuring that there will be many and sometimes major issues to be addressed when the work begins.[117]

- If the contractor is losing money because of poor job documents or mistakes in his bid, it is almost certain that quality will suffer, corners will be cut, and change orders will be inflated to make up the losses.

- On competitive bids, the "winning" bidder is often the poorest estimator, the one most desperate for work, or the one who makes the biggest mistake; any one of which means that there will be major issues to be addressed when work begins.

- Although it may seem counterintuitive, the bidding process gives the client less control over the budget and the schedule because the builder is forced to be rigid to protect his hoped-for profit.

- Often builders who have been awarded a job are required to rush through their set-up phase in order to start quickly because the design-bid process took longer than expected. Having inadequate time to prepare causes problems during construction.

- Having whittled his numbers down to win the bid, the contractor must now charge for every change in the job documents—even ones that seem insignificant to the client—to make his hoped-for profit.

---

117 Designers maintain a list of prequalified builders to bid on projects, but their efforts often have limited success. Many of the best builders will not bid competitively, some builders are too busy, some have gone out of business, some are not qualified, and some after having unsuccessfully bid with one designer will no long provide bids. Therefore, in residential work, designers often struggle to find qualified bidders and frequently circumvent the process, only making it appear to be a competitive bidding process among equals.

- If there is intense job friction or if lawsuits are threatened, some designers may be intimidated and back away from overseeing the project.

- The builder's skill and those of his suppliers, subs, and staff go unused during the design-planning process.

Advantages of DBB for the builder

- Someone else is responsible for the entire design-planning process, freeing the builder up to focus on construction.

- The builder has less liability exposure.

- A less complex organization is required.

- For a new contractor, an experienced designer may offer advice and direction that would be unavailable otherwise.

Disadvantages of DBB for the builder

- For a skilled estimator on a moderate-sized custom home, it takes 80 to 120 hours to do an accurate line item bid.[118] Assuming there are three bidders, each one has a 33% chance of success, if other bidders don't have a connection to the client or the designer, the work actually gets done, and the design firm is not simply checking prices. With few exceptions, the DBB model provides residential contractors the opportunity to bid and with little actual work to show for the effort.

---

118 If the design and construction details are not fairly standard and if the plans are not thoroughly detailed, it can take considerably longer.

- "Winning" a bid because you are willing to do the work for less than someone else—by squeezing overhead and profit, by hoping you will make it up on change orders, by planning on doing it faster than seems possible, or because you made the biggest mistake—sets your company up for a nasty work situation in which the very best outcome, although not the most likely one, is that you will squeak by with a marginally satisfied customer and a tiny profit.

- It is not uncommon in a DBB situation for bids to come back too high for the client's budget. The project may be redesigned and rebid or dropped entirely or rebid a couple of times and then dropped, wasting countless hours for each bidder. Further, because neither the designer nor the bidders start fresh, each time the project is redone the details become more muddled and the bids more guesswork than accurate information, assuring an intensely difficult project even before the work begins.

- Too often, builders find insufficient details in the job documents to do a thorough estimate,[119] and when information is missing, they must ask for it—donating still more time—or guess at what is intended, making the estimate less accurate.

- Once the contract is awarded, unless there is gross negligence or a large item has been entirely missed, seemingly small issues that are incomplete or inaccurate become the builder's problem, adding costs impossible to include in the estimate and for which he is generally unable to charge.

---

119 Most designers rely on bidders' questions to fill in a few minor details. If they are relying on them to fill in countless unanswered questions, it is a poor set of documents and the designer is taking advantage of the client and the bidders.

- When larger details are missing from the job documents, the builder may find out only as the item comes up in the construction process and then the project must be delayed while the designer "clarifies" the details—costing the builder time—or the builder develops the details himself, gambling that his solution will meet the designer's and client's approval. If it doesn't, he may end up redoing it at his expense.

- Clients often see the builder as responsible for increased costs because the clients don't understand the connection between poor job documents and rising cost and because the builder is nearly always responsible for the change orders.

- Change orders often cause intense conflict between clients and the builder because clients don't understand that they are not just paying for the item changed or added, but for discussions and meetings, disruption to the work flow, material changes, reassigning labor, rescheduling subs and supplier, profit and overhead, and many other small, unseen costs.

- If the builder has used the contract provided by the design firm without revision, he may place himself at a serious legal disadvantage because, in my opinion, he surrenders most of the authority and assumes most of the responsibility for that project. [120]

---

120 Using an AIA contract, for example. See the discussion of AIA contracts under Types of Contracts.

ENGINEERING/ ENGINEER

Engineering, the discipline of applying scientific, mathematical, and practical knowledge to the design and construction of objects.

Engineer, one who practices engineering as a profession.

Engineers are the folks who develop the technical items in residential construction: site plans, surveys, septic systems, soil tests, seismic loading, wind force, and structural designs. Geotechnical and structural engineering, subcategories of civil engineering, predominate in residential construction. Occasionally you may find a need for thermal, acoustical, mechanical, electrical, or industrial engineers.

Try not to become a man of success,
but rather a man of value.
—Albert Einstein

ENGINEERING NOTES

For centuries most of the engineering required in residential work was done by builders. Even now an experienced builder will often determine by rule-of-thumb, common sense, or a reference source the engineering required. But today using an engineer is often mandated by the need for technical expertise, building codes, or the building department.

———

When hiring an engineer understand what you are asking for. Read applicable codes. Discuss the project with a subcontractor to understand normal trade practice. Discuss parameters, standards, and options with the engineer. If the size of the project warrants it, before accepting the drawings, sit down with the sub and engineer and review the blueprints.[121]

———

Engineers sometimes cross disciplines. If they have experience in the area you need that's okay, but be certain you are not their first client for that type of work. And if you are, be sure you are not paying them to learn what they need to know.

———

There are small and large engineering firms and for most residential projects both will work. But generally, if a job is within their abilities, freelance engineers or small engineering firms will give better service at lower cost than larger ones.

———

121 I once hired a long-established local engineering firm to design a road for a housing project. Having no knowledge of what was required and trusting that because they were a well-known firm, they were good, I relied completely upon them. I learned about a third of the way through the road construction and too late to stop it that, according to the standards for residential streets, everything about the road was overdesigned by a factor of three. The added cost nearly broke the project. Out of a long list of mistakes, the biggest were that I did not vet the engineer and I did not have even the most basic knowledge of what I was asking for.

Ask these questions before hiring engineers: What types of projects do they specialize in? How much experience do they have specifically in what you need? Ask them to review with you the blueprints for two projects that are similar to yours that they have developed. Consider visiting a couple of their projects. Ask them how they will go about developing your project, what the parameters and options are, and what the final product will and will not include.[122] Ask for and call references.

_____

Many engineers can legally review and stamp residential drawings. Some building departments require construction drawings to be stamped by a licensed designer or architect, but in most cases, an engineer's stamp will meet these requirements. Of course, the drawings must still have adequate details and meet code.

_____

Make it clear that you want a practical design. Engineering design may be either straightforward or elaborate, and some engineers have both financial and artistic incentive to make it elaborate. Discuss their approach in advance to be certain they understand what you want. When the design is complete, and in advance of starting work, review the design with the appropriate trade to be certain it is not overly elaborate. If it is, have it redesigned.

_____

Roof trusses must be accompanied by the engineering calculations used to design them. These calculations must be stamped by a licensed engineer.

_____

122 In the *Journal of Light Construction*'s archives, search for articles by Harris Hyman. He is an engineer who wrote for the magazine for years and his articles address practical issues involving residential engineering.

Each engineered structural component must be stamped. Components such as a floor trusses or laminated beams, for example, must be stamped with a seal providing relevant information and indicating that they pass code. Ask your material supplier for product literature on each component and study it to learn how to read the stamp. Call the manufacturer or visit their website for further information.

HOME INSPECTION / INSPECTOR

Home inspection is the physical examination of a property to determine its current condition, followed by a written report detailing the issues and the problems that were found.

A home inspector is the individual who inspects the house and produces the report. Some states require certification or licensing for home inspectors and some don't.

In principle, a third party providing a buyer and seller with a comprehensive unbiased property inspection is a great idea. In practice, its value is often questionable. While there are skilled home inspectors with integrity and common sense, there seem to be just as many unqualified ones.[123] Given that the process is entirely subjective—that is, the opinion of the inspector—the value of the report rests entirely on their skill and integrity. I have worked with dozens of inspection reports—for both buyers and sellers—and too often I have found recommendations that are petty, wrong, or so generic as to be meaningless, leading me to the conclusion that in many cases the reports are padded to justify the fee. I have found important items missed entirely, and again and again I have noticed that some inspectors have pet peeves that cause them to focus on certain things while letting others pass without notice. And finally, home inspection contracts are filled with so many exceptions and exclusions that it makes the entire service suspect.

Therefore, when buying property, check the home inspector's credentials carefully: How long have they been

---

123 Recently, friends paid $1700 for a home inspection on a house they ended up buying. During a planned renovation, it was discovered that 60%–70% of a very large deck's framing was so rotten that it crumbled in your hand. The inspection report noted that the deck "was sound." There are countless stories like this involving home inspections.

inspecting property? Are they certified or licensed?[124] What associations are they a member of and for how long? What regular training are they involved in? How many inspections have they done?[125] What do they look for and what aren't they qualified to inspect? Call three recent clients for reference and look online to see if there have been complaints or lawsuits filed against the inspector or his firm. Read the home inspection contract with great care—note exclusions and exceptions. Review a few of the inspector's recent reports and ask lots of questions based on what you see, to understand what you can and cannot expect from a home inspection.

Typically the inspector is chosen by the buyers or their realtor and the seller has no control over the choice. But check the inspector's qualifications anyway to gain a sense of his experience and reputation and know that your only real control in this matter is how you respond to the report. If you are in a weak selling position—bad market or poor property— you may need to take care of some or all of the items in the report to make the sale. However, if you are in a strong selling position—strong market, great property—there is no reason to assume responsibility for anything in the inspection report unless it is a structural or a safety issue. A clear exception to this approach is a new or newly renovated home where part of what you are selling is the idea that nothing need be done. But even then carefully review the home inspection to understand what is reasonable and what is petty. Consider refusing to do the small stuff.

---

124 What is required varies by state.
125 It should be a minimum of 500 inspections.

HOME INSPECTION NOTES

Home inspectors do visual inspections. They do not dig along the foundation to check the waterproofing, remove siding to check for water damage, or dig into the wall to inspect insulation. Instead they extrapolate the condition of these items by looking for telltale signs of problems on the material's surface. They do open utility doors, peer into nooks and crannies, and climb around in the basement and attic. During the inspection they are looking for current defects (things like old roof shingles or a broken hand rail), items that may cause future damage (leaking pipes, bad caulking, or missing flashing), items that make the property uninhabitable (severe mold or structural issues), and safety hazards (like frayed wires or a blocked chimney flue).

———

Being a builder or tradesman does not qualify that person to do a home inspection.

———

Home inspectors do not typically check building codes, zoning, property boundaries, soils, or rights-of-way.

———

Before listing a property for sale, consider paying to have a home inspection done. This offers several important advantages: You choose the inspector. It will be obvious that you are not hiding anything. You can replace or repair those things you choose to and let people know in the listing the items that will be sold "as is." If buyers choose to have their own inspection done, there will be few surprises and, therefore, less disruption to the sales process. And it may remove the aggravation of the buyer using the home inspection report to gain concessions or lower the sales price.

———

When selling property, insist on getting the buyers' list of demands well before the closing date. State this in the contract. You need weeks or at least several days—not hours or a couple of days—to review the report, determine what to take care of, and to fix those items. Getting a report at the last minute puts the seller at a significant disadvantage as they scramble to understand what might be required and how they will respond.

———

Buyers are by definition agreeing to take over the ongoing stream of maintenance every building requires. Yet nearly every buyer—often encouraged by their real estate agent—will attempt to use an inspection report to negotiate a lower purchase price or force the seller to fix maintenance items. Unless the items are structural or safety issues or you are in a weak selling position, give away very little based on an inspection report.

———

There are inspectors who specialize in such things as septic fields, radon, soil, mold, water, energy efficiency, and leaking foundations. When items are not covered by a standard home inspection, search for an inspector specializing in what you need.

———

INSURANCE, AGENT / BROKER

Commercial insurance brokers can get quotes from several insurance companies and therefore they have more products and likely the best prices. Further, if you are dropped from one carrier, they may have another one with whom to place your policies.

Commercial insurance agents represent specific insurance companies and their primary loyalty is to the carrier. But having a more direct relationship with that carrier, they may be better able to help resolve issues in your favor.

Indemnity is compensation, protection against damage or loss.

Commercial insurance is complex and fluid. Learn as much as you can about it early in your career and manage it for the best combination of coverage and low rates. Begin by finding out which commercial brokers and agents operate in your area, which insurance companies are licensed in your state, which policies are mandatory, and which are optional but important. Ask each broker/agent to explain the options he offers and discuss the pros and cons of each. Contact your state's insurance regulators and ask how and when you might use them. Ask as many questions as required until you fully understand what you need, and once you do, put your entire insurance package out to bid to three or more brokers/agents, allowing time to collect, study, and compare the quotes before committing to an agency.

The insurance you need will vary by the type of work you do and where you operate. Here are some examples of types of insurance you may need:

General liability provides protection against your company's negligence resulting in bodily injury or property damage.

Builder's risk offers coverage for property that is under construction and protects against damage that results from theft, fire, or vandalism, and other accidental loss and damage to the property.

Workers' compensation provides compensation and medical care to workers hurt on the job.

Umbrella liability provides liability coverage above and beyond that offered in a general liability policy; it is intended to fill coverage gaps in other policies.

Inland marine provides coverage for goods in transit, on job sites, and for construction equipment.

Errors and omissions protects against economic loss from errors or omissions during design and construction.

Employment practices liability provides coverage in the event of legal actions because of employment issues such as discrimination, wrongful termination, and harassment.

Ask one or several insurance agents the following questions—and anything else you can think of—as many times as necessary until you understand the answer:

- What is a deductible and how does it affect the policy rates?

- Is the deductible per incident or a one-time yearly figure?

- What is a "hold harmless" clause?

- What types of insurance and what dollar amount of coverage does each subcontractor have to carry, and how are you affected if they don't?

- What is an "exclusion"?

- What is a bond—bid, performance, payment—when would you need one, and what do you need to qualify to get one?

- What do insurance adjusters do, and when would you dispute their judgment?

- What is "asset depreciation," and how does it affect what is paid on a claim?

- What are "policy limits," and how might they affect you?

- What will each policy cover—and what won't be covered—if a claim is filed?

- How does an insurance company decide which claims to pay and which to deny?

- When would a claim not be covered and why?

- What is a "rider," which are available to you, and which are recommended?

- What is "broad form coverage"?

- What happens to your rates and your coverage when you make a small claim, what about a big one, and what if you make two claims or three?

- What causes an insurance company to cancel policies, either for reasons related to your business or not?

- What is an "experience modification ratio"?

- What does "premise exposure" mean?

- What are "premium calculations"?

- What are product liability/completed operations?

- And what causes your rates to move higher or lower in the insurance world?

INSURANCE NOTES

Selecting a Broker/Agent

Know the difference between good and bad insurance companies. The good ones cover legitimate losses for the value of the item (minus the deductible) after confirming the claim; the bad ones begin by questioning everything and fight to pay nothing, and barring that, to pay the smallest amount possible. Research companies online and buy from the one with the best ratings. [126]

A commercial agent or broker is distinct from those who sell policies for homes and autos. Be certain that the one you choose has extensive experience with construction insurance.

Check the financial health of any insurance company you are considering. Insurance companies go bankrupt like any other business.

Look into group insurance policies. Some building associations provide group insurance policies or insurance discounts to its members. Check with the local chapters of the National Association of the Remodeling Industry (NARI) and National Association of Home Builders (NAHB).

---

126 *Consumer Reports* magazine and its website offer detailed information about insurance, and although the information is directed at private consumers, reading it will be informative.

Choose an insurance company that is licensed to operate in your state. This way, the state government will often intervene in policy disputes and may guarantee coverage if the insurance company fails.

Work with the most knowledgeable agent available. You need someone who can answer your questions, as well as the questions you don't know to ask. Interview those you are considering to learn how long they have been an agent, how long they have sold commercial insurance, how much they know about the finer points of the policies, and how many construction clients of your size they currently have.

When you get your policies, meet with your agent—a few times if necessary—to go over them thoroughly until you understand every term, every clause, in each policy. This is not fun, and some agents may resent it. However, over the course of your career you will pay an enormous amount of money for insurance; therefore, expecting coaching from your agent is perfectly reasonable.

Everything used in conducting your business should be covered in your commercial insurance policy. This includes your home office, garage, vehicles, tools, trailer, sheds, employee's vehicles that are used for work, and so on.

Consider "self-insuring" some items. To self-insure means not to buy insurance coverage for certain things, but instead, if the item it is lost, stolen, or damaged, you pay for its replacement. With tools, for example, insurance will pay the depreciated value. That is, if you paid $700 for a hammer drill two years ago and it is stolen, insurance will pay a portion (on tools, a tiny portion) of the cost to replace it. This is why for certain items it may make sense not to pay for insurance coverage.

Managing Insurance

Actively manage your insurance. Raise deductibles when the business can easily pay for what is likely to be claimed or when the risk of a loss is small. Cut unneeded coverage after carefully considering the risk of not having that policy. Check the insurance companies' "premium calculations" for errors and correct anything that is wrong. Develop a company culture that promotes safety. Periodically get competitive bids on all of your insurance needs.

Insurance does not protect against recklessness. Insurance companies will raise rates, drop coverage, or deny a claim given a reason to do so. And the industry shares information, meaning that moving to another company will become difficult or impossible for those with a bad record, and moving will not eliminate higher rates anyway because every insurance company will know about past claims. Insurance is a method of managing risk and a hedge against catastrophic loss, it is not intended to cover neglect.

Insurance will not fix your mistakes. It will not pay to fix work that was done improperly by you, your employees, or subcontractors.

Safety is the best insurance. Having an effective safety program in place helps keep the cost of insurance down. If you have an active safety program that your agent is unaware of, let him know about it.

———————

Maintain a long-term relationship with an insurance broker or agent, if you can. Insurance is complex and costly and maintaining long-term relationships and paying competitive rates may be mutually exclusive. Every few years ask other agents to bid on all of your insurance and if the rates with your current company are too high, ask for them to be reduced. If your agent can't or won't, and there is a substantial savings to be had, consider moving your policies to another company.

———————

Your questions help make your agent better. Do not hesitate to ask and expect thorough answers to everything that you need to know about your insurance policies.

———————

Ask to be shown what your insurance rates are based on. Understand the "experience modification ratio" and the "premium calculations" for each type of insurance that you carry. Some of the rates are based on your past history and some are based on judgments or assumptions about your company, and the information may be wrong. Correcting it could lower your rates, in some cases significantly.

———————

Agents/brokers are in business to make money. No matter how friendly you are with them, they are in business and, therefore, will not necessarily inform you when an insurance rate could be lower or a policy dropped unless you ask.

———————

Check regularly on changes to your coverage. Each year or each time your policies are updated, ask your agent or broker for a point-by-point written list of what has changed between the old policy and the new one so that you can easily understand the effect on your coverage. Call him to discuss the changes and ask any questions that come to mind. All agents should do this as a regular part of their service but many don't, and some will resist doing it even when asked.

————————

Meet with your broker/agent twice a year. Set aside a few hours to sit with your broker/agent to review coverage, exclusions, riders, and costs. Do you have the coverage that you need? Do you need everything you are carrying? Are policy limits high enough? Are the deductibles right? Are you paying the lowest rate possible? Laws change, insurance policies change, and as your business changes and grows, its insurance needs will change. Although a good agent will help, it is up to you to keep your insurance current.

————————

Check on the effects of a large job on your insurance rates. Each time that you bid a large job, contact your agent to learn if it will affect your rates. If it will, include the rate increase in the bid.

————————

Be sure you are covered. Ask your agent/broker to review the specifications on large and nonstandard jobs to confirm that your insurance will cover all situations specific to that project.

————————

Treat auditors well. Once a year the company providing your workers' compensation insurance will send an auditor to review your books.[127] Open your office and books to them. But don't sign off on a "workers' compensation insurance audit" until you fully understand what the numbers are based on. It may be slow going at first. You may discover that your record-keeping system must change in order to provide all that they need or to know exactly what you are being charged for. But understanding this procedure could save you tens of thousands of dollars over the course of your building career.

Keep photographic records. Take photos of your equipment, jobs in progress, office changes, anything purchased, and accidents just after they occur. Photographs will help to settle insurance claims. Devise a clear filing system that allows quick retrieval because over the years you will gather thousands of photographs. Carry a good quality digital camera with you at all times, and equip everyone in the field with simple digital cameras and teach them to take photos from various distances and angles, on all sides of the subject, and with enough light. It is rare that one has too many photographs. Periodically remind employees in the field to use the camera.

Don't misclassify workers[128] or put subs on your payroll. When the insurance company finds out—and they almost certainly will at some point—you may be liable for back charges for months or years. If the discovery happens to coincide with a claim they will have clear grounds to deny it, and they may increase your rates drastically or drop your coverage entirely.

---

127 In the Subcontractor Notes, see *Get a Certificate of Insurance …* for more information.

128 That is, claim that a roofer is a carpenter, for example, because the insurance rates for a carpenter are less than for a roofer.

Keep every subs' certificate of insurance in their file folder. Set up a system that reminds you to contact them a month before their insurance expires, if they have not renewed it themselves.

———————

Every year check driving records. Check records of everyone who drives company vehicles or their own vehicle on behalf of the company. Anyone with serious driving violations who gets into an accident while driving for the company will put it at risk of lawsuits for negligence and much higher liability claims. Have each employee or prospective hire order their own driving record—because of privacy laws, if you order it you will get limited information—and have them sign a form authorizing you to see it. If their driving record is bad or if they are unwilling to let you see their record, *do not let them drive for the company in any capacity.*

———————

There will be times that you will be required to change insurance carriers. No matter how good a risk your company is, the insurance company may drop your coverage, stop offering a certain type of coverage, double or triple its rates, or change a policy so much that it no longer meets your needs. The availability of insurance is based on a hundred factors, many of which are unaffected by the actions of your business. It could be a change in government regulations, the uncertainty around a specific issue—mold, flood, or hurricanes, for example—or an unexpected rise in workers' compensation claims. The issue may cause a single insurance company or the entire industry to withdraw from a geographical area or from offering one type of insurance. It is not personal, although it can be frustrating, inconvenient, and costly.

———————

Claims

View an insurance claim as a process of discovery and negotiation. Do not assume that what the insurance company proposes is the final outcome. In many cases, reviewing the adjusters' estimate and disputing—with hard evidence—those things that they low-balled or forgot should increase the settlement amount. If you determine that there is clearly more value than the insurance company is willing to pay and your negotiations stall, bring your lawyer into the mix. If you feel pressure to settle because you need the money, consider borrowing until the claim is settled; but borrow cautiously, the final figure may be less, in some cases far less, than you hope.

———

Do not rely on the insurance adjuster's estimate when making a claim. Instead get at least two additional estimates from independent firms—for example, a roofing company or an auto repair shop—and if their prices are higher than the adjuster's, submit the new estimates to the insurance company and expect the payout to be adjusted.

———

LAWYER, ATTORNEY

> **Lawyer/attorney**, advocate, counsel, counselor, prosecutor, solicitor, legal representative

Depending on their focus—there are dozens of categories and legal specialties—lawyers may provide advice and assistance in setting up and running companies, collecting money, resolving employee issues, writing or reviewing contracts, defending or initiating lawsuits, negotiating settlements, and in a hundred other situations. Seek a general practitioner with years of legal experience—including representing contractors if possible—and a wise and even temperament. Interview lawyers the same way you do other professionals and check with the state bar association to learn if there are complaints or disciplinary actions pending against those you are considering. Choose carefully; the right lawyer will help your company succeed.

"Integrity is telling myself the truth…honesty
is telling the truth to other people.
—Samuel Johnson

LAWYER NOTES

Know when you really need a lawyer. Consult a lawyer if you are being sued, if you are contacted by an attorney representing someone else, when you are faced with legal issues that you don't fully understand, when you are firing someone and it is contentious, when buying real estate, and when developing contracts or an employee handbook. You might also have a lawyer involved when negotiating with an insurance company, OSHA, or a workers' compensation auditor.

Many online sites give basic legal advice at little or no cost, but they should only be used to gain an overall understanding of the issues, never as a substitute for skilled legal advice.

Avoid aggressively confrontational attorneys. In my experience this attitude creates conflict and costs a great deal more than you will ever get from it. The best attorney I ever used could be tough, but he began by trying to get the best result for everyone involved, and used confrontation as a last resort. His approach offered a calming influence that went a long way toward making business relationships work.

> "Discourage litigation. Persuade your neighbors
> to compromise whenever you can. As a
> peacemaker the lawyer has superior opportunity
> of being a good man. There will still be business
> enough." —Abraham Lincoln

When you need a legal specialist, ask your attorney for a recommendation. Situations will arise that require something other than a generalist. Your attorney will direct you to someone they know and trust.

Hire lawyers based on experience, not price. Most lawyers charge by the hour and many people look for the lowest rate, but the hourly rate will often be higher for the best and most experienced lawyers because they will be faster, more skilled, and more thorough than their less expensive colleagues. Also, you may be able to negotiate a flat fee or cap for the total number of hours billed for handling a specific legal issue.

When deciding if an issue should be taken to court, negotiated, arbitrated, or let go, ask your lawyer to analyze the legal options, break the strategy into stages, estimate the cost for each, give an opinion about the likelihood of success, and outline what he believes is the best course of action. Although this process will not provide a perfect road map, nor are legal issues the only ones to be taken into account, it will provide some basis on which to make a judgment.

A lawsuit will get their attention. If another party is not taking your effort to collect money or to resolve an issue seriously, you may force their hand by initiating a lawsuit, which will cause them to spend money.

Self-justification, revenge, or anger must never be the motivation behind legal action. Each will lead you to choose the least effective alternative, no real satisfaction or advantage will be gained, and the financial and emotional cost will be far higher than any value received. Instead, look at each situation as a business equation: $2 + 2 = 4$. If this, then that. The more detached you are—that is, the less anger, frustration, righteousness, or blame you bring to a situation—the better your decision making will be and the better the outcome.

> "Before you embark on a journey of revenge, dig two graves."—Confucius

---

REAL ESTATE BROKER / AGENT

Brokers, qualifying brokers, or principals[129] are real estate agents licensed to operate a real estate agency.

Real estate agents facilitate the buying and selling of property. An agent holds a real estate license and works under the umbrella of a broker's agency. Real estate agents may also serve as property and rental managers, oversee the exchange and auctioning of property, and act as consultant to the buyer or seller of property.[130]

Property market analysis is an estimate of a property's current market value, generally done by the seller's real estate agent to determine at what price to list the property. The figure is based on the current market conditions and the property's key attributes.[131]

Property appraisal is a more rigorous and formal method of determining a property's value than a market analysis. Appraisals are done by trained and licensed property appraisers, and lenders will only use

---

129   In Oregon, and perhaps other states, the law has changed to license all real estate agents as brokers.

130   The term Realtor® is a registered trademark of the National Associations of Realtors and may be used only by their agents.

131   The figure the agent arrives at is a suggested value; it may be too high or to low. Therefore, do your own research. Understand the property's strengths and shortcomings, discuss it with a few agents, and find out what similar properties in the area have sold for—your agent will give you a list of these. Visit websites such as realtor.com and zillow.com. Consider paying an independent property appraiser (not one suggested by the agent) to work up a figure, although understand that an appraiser will often be more conservative than a real estate agent.

a professional appraiser's report to establish a property's value.[132]

Closing or settlement is the final step in the process of buying or selling property. The buyers bring money to the table (generally from a lender, deposited in an escrow account), pay closing costs, and sign legal documents— then the property is transferred into their names. The seller pays closing costs, signs legal documents, pays off the balance of loans on the property, and receives the remaining monies. The attorney or title company records the appropriate documents and the closing is complete. Details will vary by the specific circumstances of the buyer, the seller, and the property, and the state in which the closing takes place.

Closing costs are the fees paid by the seller and the buyer to transfer property. They may include title search fees, title insurance costs, loan origination fees, survey cost, credit report charges, inspection-attorney-real estate agent fees, escrow fees, and prepaid taxes and insurance payments. The real estate agent will provide an estimate of anticipated closing costs for the buyer and the seller. The items to be paid and the cost of each will vary with the specifics of the contract and the state in which the property is located. Who pays closing costs, although dictated somewhat by convention, is often a point of negotiation between the buyer and the seller.

Title or deed is the legal document that conveys title to the new buyer. A lender retains a lien on the property until the loan is paid off. Before the loan is repaid, the

132 As with an agent's property market analysis (see previous footnote), appraising the value of a property is not an exact science and there may be significant variations from one appraiser to another. If the first appraisal is lower than you and the agent expect and the property warrants it, consider paying to have a second or even a third appraisal done.

property cannot be sold or refinanced without the lender receiving payment for the outstanding loan balance. Upon payoff, the lender will convey the title to the property owner.

Title search is an examination of public records—usually done by a real estate lawyer or a title company, but it may be done by anyone—to confirm that the seller has the right to sell the property; to discover if easements or other restrictions exist on it—rights-of-way or covenants, for example—or if any liens—taxes, loans, mechanic's— are registered against the property; and to ensure that there are no other encumbrances or defects in the title. There may be documents which are not recorded in the public records that affect the property—an agreement for a property easement or a private loan are examples of items that might not be recorded—it is up to the seller to disclose these.

Title insurance may consist of two policies. The first, which almost every buyer will obtain, is an Owner's Policy of Title Insurance, which protects the buyer against irregularities not discovered in the title search, such as undisclosed easements, liens, or unpaid taxes. The second policy is required by the lender to insure that taxes are current and that the lender is protected if encumbrances are found after the property goes to closing.

Having worked with dozens of real estate agents in my career, I can't find much to recommend a profession in which there exist far too many easily exploitable—and, for all but the most experienced client, nearly impossible to detect— conflicts-of-interest. Here are a few examples:

With sellers: claiming they can get more for a property than is likely in order to get the listing, and then, when the sales agreement is signed, insisting the price must be lowered to sell it; getting to closing quickly, which offers them the highest financial reward but not necessarily the highest price for the client. There are many more.

With buyers: pushing them to choose quickly instead of finding the best property; ignoring the clients' budget and pushing them toward a higher-priced property, which provides a higher commission; recommending a lax or unqualified property inspector, which allows more properties to go to closing. There are many more.

Real estate agents have wide variations in experience, ethics, and reliability. There are new agents, part-time agents, and full-time agents with many years of experience. There are agents who work for the client's best interest and the cynics who care only about getting to closing. While an experienced agent will be more helpful in complex transactions, a new or part-time agent may have fewer clients and more time to devote to you. Your job is to find one of the really good ones. When choosing an agent, talk with their most recent clients, review online comments, and interview the most promising ones *at least twice*. Ask hard questions: are their answers informed, direct, and honest?

REAL ESTATES NOTES

Choosing an Agent

ASK THESE QUESTIONS:

- How long have they been an agent?

- How long with this agency?

- Are they full- or part-time?

- What geographical areas do they cover and are there areas they do not cover?

- Do they specialize in certain types of property?

- Are there types of property they do not handle?

- How many properties do they currently have listed?

- How many clients are they currently working with?

- How many properties have they sold (or found for clients) this month, this year, last year?

- What is their commission rate?

- Would they take a flat fee instead of a commission (if this benefits you)?

- How much would they recommend listing the property for and how long do they think it will it take to sell?[133]

---

133 It will take time to come up with an accurate figure and the answers to both of these questions are estimates, not absolutes.

- What will their marketing plan look like?[134]

- Are you expected to bear any of the advertising costs?

- Will they hold open houses and, if so, how many times and for how long?

- How will they keep you informed about what is going on and how often?

- What is the difference between an exclusive and a nonexclusive agreement?

- What would they suggest you do to the property to prepare it for selling?[135]

- What else will be required of you?

- Will they place a for sale sign on the property (they don't have to)?

———————

134 Some agents will intentionally leave the impression they will do a great deal of advertising, but in fact do very little. Therefore, insist on seeing a written marketing and advertising plan, a budget, and attach both as legal addenda to the contract along with an agreement that they will let you know each time they place ads or hold an open house and what the response was to each. The marketing plan should, at a minimum, answer these questions: Where will they advertise? How many times? How big will the ads be? How long will they run? How much will they spend on ads weekly or monthly?

135 Agents should be able to advise you on which low-cost improvements will help to sell a property. But keep in mind that all improvements make their job easier and cost them nothing. On a fairly regular basis, agents suggested "improvements" to our houses that would have cost more than the anticipated profit from the sale.

Know that a real estate agent is not your friend, confidant, or business advisor unless you have a long-standing relationship with them, and even then, be cautious.[136] Do not disclose personal or financial information beyond what is required. Take their advice as you find it useful, but do your own research and use an informed friend, an attorney, or an impartial real estate agent for advice and as a sounding board.[137]

Whomever you choose, *read the contract thoroughly*. Understand every word, sentence, and clause. Some agents will tell you that much of their contract is "boiler plate,"[138] implying or even stating that you don't need to understand it because the clauses will never be used. And, in fact, they will rarely be used, but when they are, they will cover the agent's interests more than yours. If the agent can't fully answer your questions, get the broker involved, but one way or another, get answers to every question before signing.

---

136 Friends had a close friend who happened to be a real estate agent. They asked her to find land for them and after some searching she found a piece of land that she presented as "perfect for their needs" and advised them to immediately make a full-price offer because, according to her, "it was sure to sell quickly." With a little digging, my friends learned that the property had been on the market for well over a year and that it was significantly overpriced.

137 Another friend writes the following about his experience with real estate agents: "...Unapologetically breaking promises and not returning calls was a common practice." When buying: "... Many agents...showed us a few properties, and then dropped us when it was apparent we were careful buyers... they were looking for a quick and easy sale....Agents would totally ignore our guidelines and take us to completely inappropriate properties." When selling: "My wife looked for ads that were to be placed by the agent for our apartment in the local newspapers and online, but found none. When we asked why, he assured us that there were ads, but could never show them to us."

138 "Boilerplate" is text that covers most situations without need for revision and is therefore used without modification from contract to contract.

Miscellaneous

Do not assume that property prices will rise endlessly. [139] Appreciation depends on location and condition of the property and on the local and national economies. Don't count on appreciation to correct a bad buy.

_____

Consider selling property yourself. There are often good reasons to use a real estate agent,[140] but anyone can buy or sell property, and, depending on how much time you have, the appeal of the property, your finances, and the strength of the real estate market, it may prove worthwhile to do it yourself. If you do, research the subject thoroughly and hire a real estate attorney or an independent real estate agent with extensive experience to coach you through the first few properties.

_____

You can handwrite revisions in the margin of a contract. Although not ideal, those notes are legally binding as long as they are legible, the meaning is clear, the same note is written on each signed copy, and each note is initialed by the same people who signed the original contract.

_____

Don't pay attention to current media experts or real estate agents about the state of the U.S. economy. The former are often enthusiastic boosters as the ship hits the rocks, and the latter are by charter and self-interest blind optimists.

_____

139 Not long ago (2007-8-9) there was a devastating drop in house prices in the United States. There have been many such events in our history, although most not as severe as this one.

140 One of the primary reasons to use a real estate agent may be the multiple listing service (MLS), although this is changing. In many areas, realtors will place MLS listings for a fee and many websites offer viewing access to MLS listings.

Working with Agents

Remember, the real estate agent works for you. Although the relationship should be collaborative, in the end you are the final authority.

Ask the agent for a copy of the state laws governing their profession.

Ask to see the agents code of ethics. Review it with them and ask questions as they occur to you. If an agent uses their code of ethics as a selling tool but does not actively follow it, it amounts to nothing.

Understand your options for working with an agent. Agents work with clients in various ways, as a seller's or buyer's agent or as an advisor, for example. Ask the agents you interview to explain the options and the advantages and disadvantages to each. When possible, use dedicated agents working only on the buy or sell side of the transaction, not on both sides— because they will have fewer conflicts-of-interest and their primary loyalty, after themselves, will be to you.

If you find yourself saying in answer to every question, "the agent said…" chances are you are relying too much on her advice and not enough on your own research and effort.

Be wary of using service providers whom agents recommend. Agents often have a list of appraisers, tradesmen, home inspectors, or lenders they recommend to clients.[141] But too often this creates a conflict-of-interest because the service provider's loyalty is with the agent and the prospect of repeat business, not with the client for whom they actually work. Therefore, find your own people and pay them directly.

––––––––––

Negotiate for a lower commission. The commission that agents try to charge—generally 6% of the sales price—is usually split evenly between the listing and the selling agents and the agents' brokerage firms get a percentage of their commission (typically more experienced agents keep a larger percentage). If another agent brings the buyer, the listing agent gets 1.5% of the commission, which, on a $300,000 house for example, amounts to $4500. That is, $225 per hour if the listing agent puts in twenty hours of work. There are expenses and some houses take more time, but some take less. Still, that is a nice payday, and it can be much larger: an agent who both lists and sells a property makes considerably more. Therefore in a good market with a good property there is no reason for a seller to pay more than 3–4%. On a tough sell—that is in a bad market or a hard-to-sell property—4–6% may be justified. [142]

––––––––––

141 There are laws against some of these practices, but enforcement is complex and spotty and human nature being what it is there are always new methods of gaining an advantage.

142 Some agents will not negotiate, and an agent is more likely negotiate with someone who will use them repeatedly, like a new home builder. A one-time seller is not as likely to be given a discount, but it is worth asking. The June 2010 *Consumer Reports* says to "Bargain to cut the standard 6 percent real estate agent's commission to 3 or 4 percent. Independent and RE/MAX agents are most likely to deal."

Brokers and agents cannot receive compensation from lenders or mortgage companies for referring a residential client. This is according to the federal law known as the Real Estate Settlement Procedures Act (RESPA). Commercial property is not covered under this law, but all compensation must be disclosed to all parties.

Buying And Selling

When buying or selling property, do not rely solely on the agent; do your own research. Ask countless questions. Follow every lead. Get outside advice. Always be willing to walk away.

If it is raw land:

- Does a site plan exist? [143]

  - How recently was it prepared?

  - Are utilities marked on it?

  - Are there existing rights-of-way or other encumbrances on the property?

- Find the utilities (sewer, water, electric, phone, gas, cable).

- Are there sources of obnoxious noise or smells?

- Are there prisons, dumps, low-income projects, or heavy traffic nearby?

---

143 If the property has not been surveyed with markers placed on the property boundaries, encumbrances, and rights-of-way—and you are serious about buying—consider asking the seller to have the property surveyed and these items flagged.

- Is the road public or private? Is it in good condition? Are there plans to widen it, dig it up, or extend it? Who maintains it?

- Are there problems with water (high water table, low laying or stagnant water, springs or underground streams, seasonal streams, heavy runoff, deep wells, or a great expense to bring city water to the site)?

- How is the property zoned? Are there changes to the zoning laws in the works? What restrictions do they place on the land?

- Are there any "overlay zones" that would restrict development or use that would otherwise be permitted in the zone?

- Is there a property survey? Get a copy. Are the property boundaries clearly marked? If not, ask that they be marked.

- Are there environmental issues?

- Have tests been done (soil, drainage, radon)? If so, get copies; if not, and you are serious about buying the land, pay to have the critical tests done.

- Are there trees or buildings with historical value? If so, does this restrict the intended use?

- How much site work is required (clearing, leveling, bringing in fill, retaining walls)?

- Is anything buried on the land (storage tanks, building foundations, trash, stumps, abandoned pipes or wires)?

- Contact the police department: what is the crime rate in the area?

If it is a building:

- Inspect all systems (plumbing, security, HVAC, and so on—bring in experts as needed) and examine the building with a bright light from footing to peak and in every nook and cranny.

- Ask neighbors what they know about the property.

- Get a written list of the cost of taxes, utilities (monthly and for several years back and ask each utility if there are rate hikes coming), and all other fees the owner has been paying.

- Find out if there are covenants (development or neighborhood) on the property. If so get a current copy and review it thoroughly to understand how it will affect your plans.

———————

Never convince yourself that the property you are looking at is perfect. It isn't and there are others that are just as good or better.[144] And do not act because the agent claims that it is a great deal or that you will lose it if you don't move quickly; their motive is suspect. You may lose a few properties, but move deliberately anyway because finding out key bits of information after a closing can be agonizingly expensive and you may have to deal with the consequences for years.

———————

———————

144 This is true a hundredfold when buying your first properties. You don't know enough yet to understand all of the possible downsides—of which there are many.

Agents won't necessarily show you all available properties. They may avoid properties that do not suit them: for example, properties offering a lower commission, those listed by a rival agent, those in neighborhoods they don't like, or those that are further away than they want to go. Look through the listings yourself and ask to see those properties that interest to you.

Agents often tell clients that a second party is interested in property they are considering. Sometimes it's true. It can also be a strategy to pressure the client to move quickly. When your agent makes claims like this, ask for details and proof. Do not let it pass unexamined because it will put subtle pressure on you to act before you are ready. A friend who has bought and sold real estate for many years tells his agents that if he learns they made false claims about someone else's interest in a property that he will sue them.

If an agent is aggressively pushing you toward a certain property, there may be a hidden incentive. Side agreements—a financial bonus or a vacation, for example[145]—between agent and owner are not uncommon. Always ask if there are added incentives. If you learn that there are—after you have negotiated the best price you can get—insist that the value of the incentive be deducted from the final price.

---

145 This is not illegal if the agreement is disclosed to all parties, however, there are times that such agreements go unspoken.

Put it in writing that an agent cannot commit to anything without your approval. Whether it's a new house or a renovation, make it clear that they are not authorized to promise anything—a time frame for completion, a move-in date, or paint colors—without your written approval and that, if they do, they agree to pay for all expenses associated with meeting that commitment.[146]

Contracts

There is nothing sacred about preprinted real estate contracts. Scratch out words, phrases, and clauses to which you do not agree, and write on the contract or add an addendum to modify or add items. The terms of every contract, from the simplest to the most complex, are negotiable. A good lawyer is essential in this process, especially when you are new to the business.

Include all quantifiable commitments from an agent in the contract. That is, what they say they will do to sell a property. This allows you to gauge their performance and to hold them accountable. It might include, for example, the number of times they will hold an open house or the amount they will spend on advertising.

---

146 Most agents will balk at this idea, but the point is to make it absolutely clear that they have no authority to speak for you without first getting your permission.

Include a cancellation clause in the contract. Write it into the agreement (do not accept a verbal assurance) that you may cancel the contract between you and an agent and her agency—for any reason or no reason and without penalty or cost to you—within one day of notifying them in writing. If they do their job, you will both be happy. If they don't, you can get out of the agreement quickly and find a better option. You may get significant resistance on this issue, however, you cannot afford to tie yourself to a contract that allows an agent to do a mediocre job or none at all.

―――――――

Write a contract clause making the purchase *contingent* on a specific outcome: for example, the result of a test, a survey, a study, or a line of credit. The advantage is that the property is under contract (usually, but not always, this means that no one can buy it out from under you) and, if the outcome is not what is stipulated under the terms of the contingency, you are not obligated to purchase the property. Use a lawyer to review or write this clause because the wording is critical.

―――――――

KEY ELEMENTS

ESTIMATING

> "There is no such thing as absolute value in this world. You can only estimate what a thing is worth to you." —Charles Warner

Estimating[147] is the process of working out what materials, labor, and resources are required to build a project, any project, from repairing a leaking pipe to building a dozen homes.

An estimator develops the estimate by breaking the job into its parts, working out quantities, gathering and assigning prices, and calculating the final cost to produce the work.[148]

Significantly, the synonyms for estimating are *approximate, judge,* and *workout,* not *exact, precise,* or *certain.* Estimating is science and art, fact and best judgment. The estimator is required to gather and manage an unruly stream of information about materials, suppliers, workmen, subs, clients, designers, weather, taxes, contingencies, construction methods, and government authorities. It is a messy process in which, if the

---

147 Even in the trade, people often use the words *estimate* and *bid* interchangeably, but they are distinctly different. *Estimating* is the process of working out what something will cost to build. *Bidding* is offering a fixed price to build a project in a competitive bid situation.

148 The American Society of Professional Estimators (ASPE), www. aspenational.org, is a nonprofit association that promotes construction estimating as a profession.

job documents and the estimator are thorough, there are no significant surprises, the client and designer are reasonable (or at least constrained by contract), the estimate is likely to be within 5–10% of the actual cost of construction. Good estimates provide for work to be done properly, overhead for expenses, and profit for growth. Bad estimates—that is, ones that miss items, use inaccurate costs, and do not include setup fees, taxes, contingencies, or enough overhead and profit— drain assets, demand constant special attention, and lower job quality. While it is difficult to say what a new builder must learn first, if he can't produce accurate estimates he won't be in business long enough for the answer to matter.

Types & Parts of Estimates

Each or **piece** is pricing one of something: a skylight, a door, a light fixture.

Assemble is a grouping of items, including labor and material, necessary to complete a task. For example, a plumber creates an assemble to replace a standard gas hot water heater—pan, unit, relief valve, wiring, piping, and labor to remove the old and install the new unit. Or a framing contractor creates an assemble to frame an 8' stud wall—studs, plates, bracing, sheathing, glue, nails, labor— and converts that cost into either a square foot or linear foot figure.

Square foot (SF) and **linear foot** (LF) are units of measure: total SF of siding or plywood or total LF of copper pipe or gutter and downspout, for example. SF/LF pricing is used in stick and unit estimating, but it can also be used as a standalone method for certain types of work—simple decks, blacktopping a driveway, or replacing asphalt shingles, for example—and it can be useful when providing preliminary pricing during the early stages of a project's development.

But SF/LF pricing fails quickly—and should not be used—if you don't have reliable cost data, if you are unfamiliar with the construction method, or if the site or the work is nonstandard. Other downsides to SF/LF pricing are that, if something must be added or removed from the estimate, there are few details available to adjust, and, because you are not breaking the project into it smaller parts, it is easier to miss nonstandard items.

Ballpark or **guesstimate**: Ballpark pricing is for discussion purposes only, not something to base a contract on: for example, having built many decks and after speaking with the owners to understand what they have in mind, the builder "ballparks" the cost to be $5,700. [149]

Stick or **line Item** uses each, SF, and LF and breaks the work into its smallest parts and prices each one as a line item (within reason; not counting nails or LF of caulk). A stick estimate is the most accurate type; however, they can take days or weeks to produce, depending on the size of the project, and the time is hard to justify when providing free bids. With cost-plus or T&M contracts, it is worth the effort because you know you have the work, it will produce the most accurate estimate, and the process will provide most of the required materials list and the information needed to develop a construction schedule.

Unit Estimate lists the items to be done on a project as units of construction—LF, SF, each, and assemblies—with each unit including all of the costs required to do the work. For example, an electrician might develop a unit cost for wiring a 1500 SF ranch house including labor, setup and cleanup, material, taxes, client conferences, overhead, and permits

---

149 In the Customer Notes section, see *Don't Give Ballpark Figures…*.

to build out the job.[150] Unit estimating is fast and accurate because it uses predetermined costs and prewritten specs—yours or those of a software program—to produce the estimate, although even unit estimates require customization to address the unique situations that occur on each job. HomeTech Advantage is an example of a unit cost estimating program.[151]

The best method of estimating is determined for each project and methods are often combined to meet specific needs: for example, a unit estimate might include a section using the stick method to price an elaborate gazebo if the estimator has no experience with or reliable cost figures for gazebos.

Types of Contracts

Negotiated contract has two meanings. The first is when the client and builder negotiate changes to a contract before signing; in this sense almost every contract is negotiated. The second is when the client selects the builder, instead of seeking competitive bids, and the details of the contract—type, price, payment terms, profit, and time frame, among others—are negotiated. Negotiated contracts are most often paired with cost-plus or T&M contracts and used on larger projects by more sophisticated clients with contractors they know to be honest and excellent at what they do.

Fixed-price (FP) contracts, also called flat fee, lump-sum, or stipulated-sum, provide for a fixed amount of money to do the work—arrived at through a competitive bid or a

---

150 Contingencies and profit should be added as line items at the end of each estimate, not in the unit price, because they will require adjustment to meet the circumstances of each job.

151 I find HomeTech Advantage estimating figures to be somewhat high—high is better than low—and, for reasons I have never understood, RS Means Cost Data in its various forms to be completely unusable.

negotiated contract—with the fixed price being adjusted up or down through the use of change orders. It is the contract most often used in residential construction.[152] FP contracts work best for straightforward projects when the estimator has extensive experience with that type of construction.

> **Advantages to the builder:** On medium and large projects, if the estimate is correct and the job runs well, he will make money, in some cases significantly more than expected. It requires less paper work and less interaction with the client. **Disadvantages:** If things don't go as expected, he is likely to lose money. If the job was "won" through competitive bid the builder has assumed all of the risk, and, it is likely there is not enough money to cover that. If the job documents are poor, there will be disputes about what is and is not included in the contract amount, and, because the builder needs to protect his margins against the homeowner's demands and expectations, the stress level is often high.

> **Advantages to clients:** They know in advance what the cost of the job will be, excluding allowances and change orders. **Disadvantages:** The builder will provide exactly what is stipulated or less, creative changes are limited, the stress level is often high, the likelihood of change orders is high, inflated contingencies are in the price, and, in some cases, the client pays significantly more than they might with, for example, a cost-plus contract—often even when the job went through the competitive bidding process.

---

152 When using a fixed-price contract, show clients the total cost of the work or division totals, but rarely line-item costs. The more information some clients have, the more they will quibble over pricing.

Cost-plus contracts (CP)[153]—the "plus" is overhead and profit—require the client to pay all job-related costs: material; workers' hourly rates with labor burden; professional fees; subcontractor fees; rental and equipment costs; bonds; permits; safety and incidental costs; and some insurance and taxes—plus an agreed upon percentage for overhead and profit. CP is often used when work must begin before job documents are complete—in the case of a fire or fast-tracking, for example; on high-end projects where quality, creativity, and flexibility are more important than price and when the builder is known and trusted by the client. CP contracts concisely detail which expenses are billed directly to the client and which are covered by the GC's overhead.[154]

> **Advantages for the builder**: It allows a more creative and collaborative atmosphere. It more fairly shares the risks with the client, and O&P is assured. **Disadvantages**: (although many builders do not see these as disadvantages): The client is more involved in day-to-day decision making, excellent communication skills are required, and the builder will not get a windfall if all goes well.

> **Advantages to client:** Just as with the builder, clients are more involved creatively and collaboratively. Decisions are based more on their preferences. The final cost may be less than a competitively bid fixed-price contract because the GC has not included large

153 Share the job-cost figures with clients when working on cost-plus and time & material contracts. This practice promotes trust, removes the main source of potential friction, helps to form a cooperative partnership, keeps the builder honest, and allows the client to make more intelligent choices. Some builders may consider this to be poor advice, research the idea and decide for yourself.

154 What is included or excluded from this list—that is, what is billed directly to the client and or covered by the builder's overhead—is open to negotiation; however, it is up to the builder to be certain his overhead figure covers all job-related costs not billed directly to the client.

contingencies, and the estimate is more accurate.

Disadvantages: A dishonest or unqualified contractor will cost the client a lot of extra money and provide poor workmanship—but then, this contractor will ruin any job. Clients may get excited by their creative involvement and build more than they intended or can afford. Some GCs may have less incentive to be efficient. It may require clients to have more oversight of the billing procedure. And many clients only feel comfortable with a fixed-price contract.

Time & material contract (T&M) also called labor & material, although often used in the same sense as cost-plus, T&M should be distinguished from it in this way: the builder adds his overhead, profit, and labor burden to the tradesmen's hourly labor rate and charges for all of the hours that it takes to complete the project plus material, subs, and miscellaneous.[155] T&M contracts are typically used for handyman services, building maintenance, and very small jobs because much of the work will require on-site problem solving, discussion, and running for materials; the client will often add to the work in progress; and the job may not justify a pre-work site visit or developing job documents. Although not common, T&M is sometimes used on larger jobs.

Advantages to the builder: He has no risk, his O&P are assured, and often the work can begin immediately. **Disadvantages**: If the job documents are poor or the clients do not trust the builder, it can create contentiousness. If the price runs up too much—that is if it exceeds the customers' expectations—the clients may feel they are being taken advantage of and refuse to pay the bill or negotiate for every dollar they owe.

155 O&P may or may not be added to material, subs, and miscellaneous items depending on the GC's policy and what was negotiated.

Advantage for client: They get the same atmosphere of collaboration and creativity as with cost-plus. There is less need for detailed job documents, work can start more quickly, and the builder is available to do whatever the client wants. **Disadvantages:** Clients assume most of the risk. A lousy builder will cost them money, aggravation, and poor workmanship, and they will have little recourse.

American Institute of Architects (AIA) produces a family of construction contracts and documents for the construction industry. I believe that if they are used in residential construction at all, it should be only on the largest projects by the most sophisticated builders because to use them properly one needs a lawyer and construction manager for advice and an office staff to carry out the requirements. Further, I believe they leave the builder financially and legally at a significant disadvantage.[156]

> "I can tell you that as an arbitrator on many construction related projects, the AIA contracts are no better and often much worse than contracts created by the contractor. …Keep in mind that AIA docs were written by attorneys who were paid by architects to create documents that protect the architect first and the contractor last."
> —Michael C. Stone[157]

---

156   Having used AIA Contracts at several points in my career, I decided that because AIA regularly revises its contracts and because its website claims its documents are fair to all parties and suitable for any sized project, I needed to re-read the contracts most likely to be used by small builders as I wrote this section; I found even more complexity and legalese than I remembered.

157   From an untitled article, see Construction Programs & Results, http://www.markupandprofit.com/construction-business-success.html.

AIA CONTRACT NOTES:

Before bidding on a project requiring an AIA contract, study the contract documents closely and ask your lawyer for advice. If there are clauses you cannot agree to, discuss the changes you require with the clients or designers to be certain they will agree to the revisions, and if they won't, think hard about passing on the work. If you do agree to bid using an AIA contract, add significant fees to comply with the complex, frequently vague, and often discretionary items that may be required.[158]

––––––––––

Never involve designers in the selection of subcontractors. Some designers require that the GC give them a list of the subs bidding on a project and the amount of their bids because they want to be involved in the sub selection process or even require that the lowest-priced subs be selected. It is difficult to imagine a more cockeyed clause in a contract. The GC is *legally responsible* for each sub's performance and a key part of what he brings to the table is a working relationship with good subs. If subs are selected on misguided criterion, the GC is guaranteed a long difficult project with a questionable outcome. Unless there is a compelling reason to include the designer or the client in the sub selection process—and not a single one comes to mind—they should never be involved.

––––––––––

158 See http://www.aia.org/aiaucmp/groups/aia/documents/pdf/aias076346. pdf, the "AIA Contract Documents Suggested Retail Price List," for a list of the available contracts. To get a feel for the contracts that a small builder might be required to use review AIA contracts A101, A102, A105, A201, and A401.

Builders who understand the cost of complying with AIA contracts may lose bids because their price appears to be high. Bidders who don't fully understand what is required often bid too low.

———————

Architects develop a small percentage—an estimated 1–2%—of the residential work done in the United States each year.

———————

When contract payment is based on a designer or someone other than the client certifying that a phase of construction is complete payment can be delayed for weeks or, in extreme cases, months, unless you meet precisely that party's definition of complete.

———————

Contracts have endless variations and on larger jobs those variations are often complex. Here are a few examples of fairly standard variations.[159]

> **Cost-plus a fixed fee:** the actual amount of O&P is agreed to in advance and does not change regardless of changes to the cost of the project.

> **Cost-plus a percentage:** the percentage to be charged for O&P is agreed to in advance with the total O&P fluctuating as the cost of the project changes.

> **Cost-plus a percentage up to a maximum fee:** a maximum figure is agreed to for O&P for the base cost and it cannot go above this regardless of the final cost of the job as described in the original job documents. If the base cost is lower, the O&P charged to the client is also lower.

159 I'm not advocating these, simply providing examples. Before agreeing to any nonstandard contract changes, carefully think through how they will affect you and consider talking with your accountant or lawyer.

Guaranteed maximum price, also called not-to-exceed or upset price: typically used with cost-plus or T&M jobs when clients require a price over which the job will not go. Essentially they are asking for the advantages of a cost-plus contract with the safety of a fixed-priced contract. The base cost of the job does not change because of errors, omissions, or overruns on the part of the GC but does change through change orders.[160]

---

160 In order to make the client comfortable and get the work, a GC might agree to a guaranteed maximum price, but only if the job details are extremely clear, the base price includes significant contingencies, and COs with O&P are used religiously.

Ways in which Jobs Are Contracted

The following list provides an overview of how small, medium, and large job contracts are typically handled, although there is a lot of variation and overlap.

Small jobs involving single trades, handyman services, and tiny projects:

- Where the specs are unknown until the work begins— handyman services or finding a short in a wire, for example—the work is rarely bid. Instead, it is done using a time & material billing method. Usually only one tradesman will be called.

- When details are reasonably standard—replacing an air conditioning condenser or plumbing a tub, for example—trades generally provide the job specs and estimate for free. They will include an amount to cover the cost of providing the specs and price in their proposal. One or a few companies may be called.

- When details are more complex—a new air conditioning or security system—each trade generally provides the job specs and estimate for free. Several bidders may be contacted. On more complex projects, one company may be paid to develop the job documents.

Mid-sized jobs involving a trade or general contractor: for example, flooring, plumbing a bath, landscaping, a small addition, or finishing a basement:

- Single service trades—flooring or pouring a slab, for example—usually develop specs and a free bid for clients and GCs, although they may not share the details used to develop their pricing. Occasionally if a project is especially complex, trades may charge for design and estimating or provide those services for a commitment that they will be given the work. A few firms might be contacted, and the cost to provide the specs and estimate the work are included in each proposal.

- Jobs with several components, such as a small addition or finishing a basement:

  - A lone GC develops the job documents at no cost and provides a free bid with the hope of being given the work. The GC—hopefully—includes the cost for these services in the proposal.

  - Clients ask several GCs to design and bid and then choose the one they like best without paying anything for the services provided. Each GC includes the cost for these services in his proposal as well as a portion of the cost for those jobs he bid on but did not get.[161]

  - A GC charges for developing job documents, and the client uses these to solicit bids. A partial or full rebate is sometimes offered if the GC who developed the documents gets the work.[162]

  - A design-build firm charges for developing the job documents, prices the work, and negotiates to do it, although occasionally the design may be put out for competitive bid.[163]

161 These first two examples are the worst possible situations for builders—and clients, too, although it is nearly impossible to explain why to a client who believes this is the way to do it—and should be avoided.

162 The distinction here is tricky. Many small builders do not market or think of themselves as design-build firms yet they develop simple documents for a deck or bath renovation, for example. As you begin in business, do not give away this key part of your service. Instead: have the client commit to you before developing the documents and include the planning costs in the price; sell planning as part of the process and charge for it up-front; find a designer to recommend; or only work on projects with existing job documents.

163 It is up to firms developing the job documents to do them in such a way that the client ends up working with them. If their planning work is put out to bid, the firm should be paid in full for their service, not simply hope that the client gives them the work.

- Jobs with more sophisticated requirements: raising a roof or a kitchen renovation, for example:

  - A design-build firm charges for design, job documents, pricing, and negotiates to do the work, although the client may sometimes put the documents out to bid.

  - A specialty firm charges for design, job documents, pricing, and negotiates to do the work, although the client may put the documents out to bid.

  - A designer or design firm charges for developing the job documents. The client either puts the work out to bid or negotiates with a GC to have it built.

Large jobs involving a design/build firm or a general contractor: an addition/renovation or new home for example:

- A design-build firm charges for developing the design, job documents, and estimate. It would expect to get the work, but the job may also be put out to bid using the firm's documents.

- A design or specialty firm develops the design and job documents charging for its work and the job is put out to bid—the designer may or may not manage the bidding process—or the client negotiates with a builder to do the work on a cost-plus or fixed-price contract.

- Stock plans for a new home are purchased and the job is bid or negotiated.[164]

---

164 In my experience, stock house plans *always* require significant work to correct and clarify them before they can be used.

ESTIMATING NOTES

Principles

There is no such thing as a perfect estimate.

On large jobs, good documents are essential to produce an accurate estimate. No one, no matter how long they have been building, can produce reliable estimates without them.

Every residential building project is unique: combining materials, methods, and designs in a shifting assortment of size, layout, location, people, and codes; that is what makes estimating and planning so difficult, but it is also what makes building so much fun.

Estimating is not hard but doing it well requires certain things: undisturbed blocks of time, thoughtful organization of the process, attention to detail, knowledge of the site and the construction method, good job documents, and time to study them thoroughly.

Read books, take classes, and begin estimating small jobs. Ask someone who does it well for advice and perhaps even training. [165]

---

[165] Before you ask a friend for help, be certain he is a good estimator: it will take a long time to unlearn bad habits. Local building associations and community colleges often have estimating classes. See Estimating Books & Software in the Bibliography.

Software helps, but it does not replace the estimator. Estimating software provides a format for specs and costs and it helps to produce clear and accurate estimates. But regardless of how advanced the program, a knowledgeable estimator is required to define the tasks, figure and adapt quantities, confirm costs, and adjust the specs.

> "…so it will come as no surprise to suggest that the pencil and computer are, if left to their own devices, equally dumb and only as good as the person driving them." —Norman Foster

Do extensive research before choosing an estimating program. Ideally you will end up using the same program for your entire building career, increasing its value to you with each passing year.

The most accurate cost information comes from your own job records. Depending on several factors—location, subs, and efficiency, for example—each company's cost will vary to produce the same item; therefore, maintain an accounting system that allows comparison between the original estimate and the actual cost as tracked in the field and that provides an efficient way for the estimator to access this historical data.

Create and customize a lifelong estimating "master list." Estimating programs allow the user to change and add to the line items provided so that over time the information can be customized to become exactly what your business needs by eliminating (or hiding) categories you don't use, adding ones you do, and incorporating your own notes and cost data.

Estimates should be done without the immediate pressure of needing work, which is why developing and sustaining a sound marketing program—even when it appears that you have enough work—is so important.

Ignoring or passing over what you don't understand in job documents will be costly. Follow and research every item to its logical end. Guessing what an item costs works sometimes—and it is better than leaving it out entirely—but the times that it doesn't work will be painful.

Do not price jobs based on what you think your competition will charge. Sell service and quality, not price.

Increase the percentage you charge for profit when the market is strong. When things slow down, decrease profit as required back to a base line figure below which you never go.

Ignore cost figures provided by whoever developed the job documents. Cost figures from designers and engineers are notoriously low because they are not professional estimators and because they have a built-in conflict of interest: a low initial estimate may encourage the client to go ahead with the project. Over and over again you will find designers' estimated costs are 30, 40, even 100% below the actual cost to build the project. Therefore, disregard their price—if possible avoid learning what it is until done with your estimate—and work up your own numbers every time.[166]

---

166 This is especially important for new estimators. Being unsure of their estimating abilities, too often their final number will match the designer's pricing.

Even in economic slowdowns, do not discount your profit by much. Residential builders, both old and new, will sometimes cut prices to get work, telling themselves that they will make it up later. Most never do. Job and overhead costs are fixed—unless efficiency can be increased—and profit is the lifeblood of the company and should be given up grudgingly.

Track the cost of materials to keep your estimates current. There are various sources of information on the web,[167] and many suppliers send out monthly price updates to their customers. Once you have established pricing sources, it will take very little time to track the costs that affect you.

Typically it takes weeks or months for a sales call or a bid to turn into a job. Take this into account when choosing which work to pursue and which to pass on.

If you are getting every job you bid, you are not charging enough. If the folks looking for "a deal" regularly select you, you are not charging enough. If you are using money from one job to pay costs on another, you are not charging enough. If you don't have enough money to pay your bills and to put some in the bank at the end of a job, you are spending too much or you are not charging enough.

Estimating can be a career choice. The skills required to produce good estimates are in demand and one can spend an entire career as an estimator.

---

167 A couple of examples: http://www.bls.gov/home.htm, http://enr.construction.com/economics/materials_trends/.

It is possible to hire an estimator or to use an estimating service. But don't do either until you can do an estimate yourself and understand the procedure and what it takes to create an estimate. If you use an in-house estimator—no matter how much experience he has—never allow an estimate to go out without reviewing it, asking questions, and double-checking the figures.

Creating an Estimate

Design firms typically provide GCs with one to three sets of drawings at no cost. They charge for additional sets or require each GC to print what they need from electronic documents or paper copies.[168] When GCs have to pay for job documents, most charge their larger subs for what they need. Some GCs print fewer sets and ask vendors to turn over their bids quickly so the job documents can be passed along to the next vendor.

Print enough job documents to provide one for each major sub, a couple for suppliers, and three for your office. The office sets are used as follows: one for smaller vendors to come to the office and do their takeoff, one for the estimator, and one for the field, assuming you get the job. Mark the estimating and field copies in several places in bold letters "ESTIMATE COPY" and "FIELD COPY"—never loan them to anyone—and file the copies containing markups and notes with the job records whether you get the work or not. If you do get the job, you will typically need two or three sets for the building department.

---

168 Local printers, Kinko's, and large stationery stores will print, collate, and staple blueprints and specs from paper copies or electronic documents.

Electronic plans can simplify estimating. Some design companies transmit plans electronically and some GCs, subs, and suppliers can do electronic takeoffs using Adobe Acrobat or other software. Digital plans allow the GC to send only that portion of the document relevant to each vendor, which in turn allows the vendor to print out just what they need or to do their takeoff on the computer. But some plans are not available electronically, and many subs and suppliers are not equipped to receive electronic plans or do takeoffs this way; therefore, you end up doing a combination of digital distribution and printing for subs and suppliers.

———————

When preparing for an estimate, it is better to gather too much information than not enough.

———————

Factor weather into your estimates. Job requirements change in winter and summer. For winter work in cold climates, take into account a source of heat, longer times for working outdoors, time for weather delays or days lost entirely, and costs for shoveling and plowing snow and covering work to protect it from snow and ice. In summer, provide for fans, ice and water, and rain and sun protection for both the crew and the building.

———————

Begin estimates soon after visiting a job site. It's best to start the same day, but definitely begin within a few days because details are easily forgotten or confused with other jobs.

———————

Have one estimate open on your desk at a time. It is too easy to confuse information if you are working on more than one job. When you have gone as far as you can with that one estimate, make notes and a to-do list so that you know where to restart, put the first estimate away and, only then, begin work on another estimate.

———————

Study the job site in preparation for doing an estimate. Notice if there are trees or stumps to be removed, power lines, trash on-site, old foundations, basement window, decks, a water spigot, or an electric outlet. Will the neighbor's fence, trees, or shrubs be affected by or affect the job? Can a backhoe get in to dig the footings or a concrete truck to pour the foundation? Is there room to pile excavated dirt? Where will incoming materials be stored? How will trash be stored and removed? Could there be an issue with theft? Is your work going to affect an existing item that will require fixing: siding or landscaping, for example. Notice and take notes and photographs of everything that might affect the construction process.[169]

Get all pricing in writing. Subs and suppliers—even those you use often—will sometimes provide verbal prices or product information that is wrong, and they may or may not take responsibility for their mistake; therefore, get written confirmation from every source for pricing and product information when developing an estimate.

Follow a well-defined estimating procedure every time:

- Familiarize yourself with the job site, plans, and specs.

- Study the job documents, highlight and note key points.

- Lay out the estimating tools: legal pads, construction index, cost data (computer or book), estimating form (computer or paper), lead pencils, eraser, colored

---

169 See Site Visit Check List in the Appendix for a basic list of what to look for when visiting a job site. Also, Byggmeister Design-Build will share its "Construction Document Review Checklist." The list and the accompanying article can be found on the website, http://byggmeister.com/.

pencils and highlighters,[170] printing calculator, engineer and architectural rulers, phone and contact list, tables of square and cubic measurement, table of architectural symbols (usually on the plans), site notes, and photographs.

- Decide what subs and suppliers will be required and what will be done in-house.

- Develop lists of questions for the client, designer, subs, suppliers, and others and get them answered; repeat.

- Use a construction index to divide the job into sections, in the order construction will proceed. Focus on the first item, break it into component parts, and "see" in your mind how the work will be done.[171]

- Consider the time, material, and equipment required for each task, assign a cost to each using a cost database, your own knowledge, subs' bids, and suppliers' prices, and move to the next item, and then the next.

Use a printing calculator or an electronic spreadsheet. Make notes alongside the figures to remind you what the numbers relate to. File this information with the estimating paper work.

Use architectural and engineer's rulers. Although it is possible to use any ruler or tape measure to scale off a drawing, architectural and engineer's rulers are scaled to match the scales used on blueprints, and they are easier to read, thus reducing takeoff errors.

---

170 Many estimators develop a colored pencil or highlighter coding system to markup and organize information for estimating. But don't get carried away; an overly elaborate system is more confusing than helpful.

171 The ability to visualize the construction process will develop to a surprising degree as you practice it.

Most architectural plans have a note that says "do not scale off drawings." This means that the designers do not want the guy in the field to determine a dimension by measuring off of the drawing because it can be inaccurate. It also lets them off the hook if you scale off the drawing and what you build is wrong. But many times, there is no choice. Either the required dimension is not on the drawings or it is wrong. If time allows, call the designer to get the dimension, but if this does not work and you must scale off the drawings, check several other points to confirm the dimension.

Use a computer program to file addresses, phone numbers, and contact notes. And when possible make it sync with everyone's phone so that the information is consistent and available to everyone.

Sometimes suppliers and sub will provide guaranteed costs on specific items for a set period of time. For example, lumber prices, supplying and installing gutters and downspouts, or installing electrical outlets. For smaller jobs, these figures may be used instead of calling each time for pricing, but use them carefully because every job has its own issues and oddities. If you are uncertain, call the supplier or sub for confirmation.

Confirm pricing from a sub or supplier for every estimate. Unless you have guaranteed pricing (see previous note), check with them because small changes will reduce your profit margin while large ones might eliminate it entirely.

When estimating, make short explanatory notes attached to each item. Explain what the figures are based on, what assumptions were made, what potential problems were found, and any contingencies allowed for. In theory, an estimate should be so well organized and notes so clear that another estimator could step in and complete the work without you being around; in practice, this is nearly impossible, but worth aiming for.

––––––––––

Pay close attention to these terms—*as needed, typical, equal,* and *match existing*—in plans and specs. Each is shorthand that saves the designer time because it reduces the number of details required. For example, when door trim is labeled "typical," the estimator and builder are being told that all similar doors are to be treated in the same way unless there is a note saying otherwise. The problem is that using *as needed* or *equal,* for example, may allow the designer not to fully think through what is required, and thus often, unforeseen issues and costs arise around these terms. Further, in the case of *match existing*, it might be impossible to match the existing material or method of construction, or the cost to do so astronomically high. Therefore, each time you run across these terms and ones like them follow where they lead, ask each question that arises, and insist that the answers are in writing; that is, do not accept a verbal response. If you can't get satisfactory answers, make the item an allowance or specifically exclude it in the proposal.

––––––––––

Be aware when material prices are volatile. There will be times when the price of commodities—lumber, roofing, metal, or concrete, for example—are changing quickly. When this happens, include their cost in estimates as either a fixed cost for only as long as the sub or supplier will hold that price or as an allowance figure that will be adjusted when the item is purchased. You cannot give a fixed price to frame a house, for example, when the cost of the lumber is changing rapidly.

———————

Estimates are done in waves as information is gathered and the details teased out, analyzed, and assimilated. On large jobs, it usually takes several passes before arriving at a final figure.

———————

When "buying out" a job—that is, making final decisions about where to purchase materials or which subs to use—try to buy as many items as possible below the estimated cost. But if you have promised—or even indicated—that you would give the order to a specific vendor, it is not the time to renegotiate or buy from someone else. Honor your commitments—because it is the right thing to do—but also because if you don't, the next time you need a price, it is likely the sub will tell you to go pound sand.

———————

Round up to the nearest whole unit of measure when estimating. If a slab measures 24' 7" × 36' 9" round up to 25' × 37'. Round $30,498.28, up to $30,500. This saves time, helps avoid mistakes, provides a small margin of error, and gives effectively the same result.

———————

Add the cost of taxes, permits, and fees to every estimate.

———————

Include taxes, mobilization, overhead, profit, contingencies, and special situation costs as individual line items in each estimate. Do not lump them into a single category. By listing them individually, you can adjust them to meet the specific circumstances of the job, you are less likely to forget them, and you can refer to them when estimating future projects.

———————

Have someone check your estimate. *Never submit an estimate without at least one other knowledgeable person reviewing the content and checking the math.* Estimating is complex and it is far too easy to make a mistake. If you do not have someone knowledgeable to review it, go over it item by item with an employee or spouse, talking through how you arrived at your figures and having them ask questions. After the initial review, set it aside for a few days and review it one more time before submitting it.

———————

Don't create an estimate and then massage the figures to lower the price. There is no point in carefully estimating a project and then randomly changing it to get work. Learn to estimate well enough that you trust your figures.

———————

Save and file all job-related documents when an estimate is complete. It is impossible to know which bit of information will be important, so save everything, whether you get the job or not. If you don't get it, some of the information may be used for future estimates. If you do get it, you will use the information to create the contract and schedule and to remind yourself of things forgotten. If the job is delayed and then restarted, you will need to review the file. And if legal issues arise, this information will be invaluable.

———————

Estimates and Clients

Don't be defensive when submitting an estimate. If you have taken the time to do a thorough estimate, don't rush to justify it if the customer appears surprised by the price. Give your price and let the response go by without reaction. If you are the first to submit an estimate, the clients' reaction may reflect their surprise at the high cost of construction. If they have other prices and yours is much higher, don't be too quick to assume that yours is wrong. If appropriate, acknowledge that you need to review your number. If upon review you believe it is correct, stand by it. If in checking, you find a mistake, correct it, but in most situations you will not be able to resubmit the bid because this would give you an unfair advantage.

Don't rush estimates. If clients come to you insisting they need an estimate quickly, explain that although you would like to look at the work—if you would, of course—a thorough and accurate estimate takes time. Give them a time frame within which you are comfortable producing their estimate, and if they insist that it must be sooner, pass on the work. Hurried estimates are filled with mistakes, costing you money and aggravation and, almost by definition, creating a dissatisfied customer.

Clients pay for extras, changes, and revisions, including overhead and profit. Don't give away work because you are happy to have the job, you feel guilty about the high cost of construction, or you believe there is "plenty of money" in the bid (I guarantee you there is not as much as you think there is).

Remove only base costs—not O&P—if, before work starts, a client removes parts of a project won through a competitive bid. It took time to produce the bid and it will take more time to make the changes; you should be paid for this effort.

BIDDING

> "There is hardly anything in the world that some
> man cannot make a little worse and sell a little
> cheaper, and the people who consider price only are
> this man's lawful prey." —John Ruskin

Competitive bidding, often called simply bidding**,** is a
process in which GCs, trades, or specialty firms are asked
to submit proposals stating what they would charge to
construct a project based on the job documents, which
may consist of specs for a single item or 100 pages of
details. These documents serve as the sole source details,
thus insuring that each bidders' estimate is developed
using the same information.[172] The client then chooses
among the bidders, and the parties sign a contract.[173]
While nearly every job requires an estimate, only some
are put out for competitive bid.

I don't like bidding. I am plagued by the image of clients
holding out work to discover who is willing to perform the
most tricks to "win" it. Competitive bidding is based on the
ideas that each job is not unique, that all builders have the same
knowledge and provide the same service, and that estimating
is an exact science and thus it is possible to fine-tune the price
just low enough to win the work and still provide good service,
a quality product, and make a profit. The premise is naïve
and illogical. The larger and more complex the job, the less
bidding serves anyone's best interests. For skilled and honest
builders and their clients, a far better option is a negotiated
contract because it most fairly meets everyone's needs and it

---

172 When a client calls a few window installers, for example, to get prices,
this is usually called getting "bids", although it isn't, because each company
provides its own details and specs, comparing their prices has little or no value.

173 This is the simple version. Depending primarily on the size of the job,
there are many variations on how work is contracted. See Ways Jobs Are
Contracted in the estimating section.

provides the best process and result.[174] If the builder is known to the client they can slip comfortably into this relationship; if not, they must take the time required to learn about each other.

And yet, as a new contractor you will almost certainly be required to bid competitively to get work. Therefore, use this time to refine your estimating and sales skills, hire excellent people, establish and fine-tune systems and policies, and build a reputation that allows you to negotiate work instead of giving away your knowledge and time.

"So, a while back, when the market was strong, I decided to reward myself for all the work I'd put into developing a top-notch crew and an exceptional client base. My reward was to stop bidding…"
—Paul Eldrenkamp[175]

---

174 If the bidders are not skilled and honest to begin with, having them bid against each other is not going to help the client in any way. Further, the best builders are usually eliminated in a selection process based on cost.

175 See "Farewell to Competitive Bidding" and "Charging for Estimates," both by Paul Eldrenkamp in *The Journal of Light Construction* archives.

GUIDELINES FOR COMPETITIVE BIDDING

Determining the likelihood of winning a bid is not an exact science, but the more you do it the more meaningful your appraisals will become.

- Does the work fit your expertise, schedule, and geographical area? Are you comfortable bidding this type of work? Is your crew comfortable doing this work? Do you have the necessary equipment?

- Are there specs and drawings? Who developed them and are they thorough and accurate? If there are no documents, does the client expect to pay for design, specs, and estimates or will they ask each company to develop its own?

- Is there a realistic budget? If not, when the bids come back too high, the client is likely to revise the project and ask for another round of bids—or decide not to do the work at all.

- Who provides the contract? If it is not your contract, ask to review it: Is it fair? Does it require more administrative or submittal tasks than normal? Are there nonstandard clauses? Do the payment terms allow for cash flow and prompt payment? How long is the final payment delayed? Does it require penalties? Is the client or designer willing to add, remove, or rewrite sections to meet your requirements?

- Are bonds required, what types, where will you get them, and do you have time to arrange for them before the bid is due?

- How much insurance is required? Are there nonstandard insurance requirements and can you fulfill them?

- How many bidders will there be? Who are they and do you know them? If not, do your homework: Are they roughly the same size as your company (bigger, higher price; smaller, lower price)? Do they tend to bid high or low? Are they busy (likely to bid high) or desperate for work (likely to bid low)? Is this the type of work they typically do? Is it worth bidding with more than three bidders (generally not, unless you have an inside-track, and if you do, you should negotiate for the work not bid it)? Are any of your competitors related to the client or have they worked with the designer before (if so, they have an inside-track)? Are they from the area (if not, their overhead will be higher and it will be harder to manage the job)? What sort of reputation do they have?

- Are the clients reasonable and fair? Are they primarily interested in service, price, quality, speed, handholding, or directing the work? What past construction experience do they have, was it good or bad and what expectations or reservations do they have because of it? Do they seem wary? Are they friendly and open? Do they complain a lot? Do they get along with each other? Are they respectful of everyone involved? Are they someone you want to work with?

- Have you worked with the design firm or know their reputation? If not, do your research: Are their job documents thorough? Do they work as equals or are they dictatorial? Are they reasonable and fair? When errors arise, do they take responsibility or blame others? Do they respond to questions thoroughly and quickly? What level of service did the client buy from the designer—that is, how detailed are the drawings and how involved will they be during construction? How will their involvement affect your bid price and work schedule?

———————

"We bid for architects, but only if there are three or fewer bidders, and only if we have the opportunity to meet the owner in person."
—Randy Polombo

"We are trying to break the habit of detailed bidding. As a design-build firm, we will give preliminary pricing, but if we are not selected to develop the project, we bow out."
—Mike Weiss

BIDDING NOTES

Principles

It is an industry joke that when the lowest priced bidder wins the job, the first question he asks is "what did I miss?" One builder I know calls the winning bidder "the first loser" since so often he is the one who made the biggest mistake.

> "Bid opening, a poker game in which the losing hand wins." —Anonymous

---

What can be earned on a job is limited, what can be lost is nearly without limit.

I don't know why so many GCs provide free bids. I do know that the strongest companies avoid competitive bidding because in so many ways it is a losing proposition that rewards the unlucky and the ill-prepared.

> "The building and remodeling industry has, for reasons lost in time, created its own tradition of free estimates. Every builder soon discovers that a whole lot of time goes straight down the tubes on estimates that never pan out into contracts." —*JLC,* 2001

All bids tend to be higher in a strong market. Even the lowest bid in a competitive bid may be significantly higher than in a slower market because builders charge more when they are busy.

Use the term *proposal* instead of *bid* when charging for estimates/bids.

––––––––––

Consider charging for estimates/bids when starting out. Even a nominal fee—in the $25 to $200 range—will eliminate tire kickers and the folks gathering information to do the work themselves. The folks calling six companies for prices will likely scoff at the idea of paying. They are not your demographic. Referrals, personal contacts, and those with whom you have met and explained your service will usually be willing to pay for your time.

––––––––––

A few companies may get 30% to 40% of the bids they submit. Most don't even get that. Put another way, companies fully committed to bidding waste 60% to 70% of their effort. And, because so often it is the company that shaved margins or made the biggest mistake that wins the job, often there is no profit left in them anyway.

> "I came to see that the challenge in pricing lies not just in winning jobs, but in winning jobs that will make money." — Bob Hanbury

––––––––––

Process

Every successful bid is based on accurate documents. It doesn't matter if it is a small job with a few specs or a large job with a full set of job documents. If the information is inaccurate or incomplete, bidders are guessing and comparing prices is meaningless.

––––––––––

Bidders must be of a similar size and abilities. A guy working out of his truck will have lower prices, and may do excellent work, but he cannot provide the same range of services or abilities as a company with an office, equipment, and supervisory and field staff.

───────────

Know your competition. Design firms and clients usually attempt to prequalify bidders, that is, invite financially sound companies of approximately the same size and capacity. But not everyone does and those that do are often forced to lower their standards to get enough bids, which is why it is up to you to know the other bidders to determine if there is a real chance of getting the work—or if you are simply donating your time.

───────────

Excessive change orders are most often caused by poor job documents.[176] Poor documents happen because the client was unwilling to pay for complete documents or the designer did a poor job. If it is the designer, the client hired badly. If it is the client trying to save money, the designer should have passed on the work. You must either charge for your time to complete the documents or pass on the work.

───────────

When competitively bidding, if you can't get answers to your questions, provide an allowance for each item without enough detail to develop a fixed price and exclude items that don't have enough details to develop an allowance. Include notes in your bid documents explaining what you did and why.

───────────

176 The other possibilities are clients who change their mind often, a builder or trade who is trying to pad the job to make up for a low bid, or unanticipated circumstances.

Clients

Clients are less likely to put jobs out to bid if they have a relationship with a company they trust. They are also more likely to negotiate the contract. This is one of the reasons it is so important to stay in touch with past clients.

> "I don't bid jobs that are not referred by a previous
> client or someone who knows us. And I don't bid
> on jobs that have more than three other contractors
> looking at it." —Sue Cosentini

If you are confident in your price and a client asks "why is your bid so high," suggest that a better question might be why is the low bid so low and how will it affect the service and the quality of the other bidder's work when they realize their mistake?

In order to get bids, potential clients will often tell builders they are looking for quality, not the lowest price. But when the process is complete they accept the lowest bid, often when it is too low to do the work. Generally, it will not help to explain that expecting a quality product with insufficient resources defies logic. When they have gone through the excruciating process of trying to get what they thought they were paying for, perhaps they will understand, although many still don't get it.

> "Price is what you pay. Value is what you get."
> —Warren Buffett

Clients often use the competitive bidding process to educate themselves. Ostensibly competitive bidding is about who will do the work for the lowest price—and sometimes it is—but clients (and designers) will often say they will not choose the lowest-priced bidder, but the best one, which is what they should do. But, if that's the case, why take up the time and resources of several bidders when they are not actually looking for the lowest cost? Because they get an education, they receive wide-ranging ideas and suggestions, they learn if they can afford to do the work, they may get free specs and designs, they can check the price of a preferred builder, and finally they get to weigh each bidder and select one. And this costs the clients almost nothing in effort or money.

––––––––––

Clients talk themselves into accepting bids that are too low. In the bidding process when one bid comes in much lower than the others, some clients see it as a boon instead of realizing they will lose far more in quality, service, and peace of mind than they will gain in price. Are clients so naïve that they believe the too-low bid is going to provide the same product and service as a complete one, or are they simply hoping they will get lucky? For those bidders whose number is right, it is baffling and frustrating, and it happens far too often.

––––––––––

MONEY

> "It is pretty hard to tell what does bring
>   happiness; poverty and wealth have both failed."
> —Kin Hubbard

MONEY DEFINITIONS

Money is what is used as a medium of payment in the form of cash, checks, and credit cards.

An asset is money in a mattress, a checking or savings account, a bond or a stock, and that portion of property, inventory, equipment, or receivables that we don't owe anything on. For example, if you own a property valued at $100,000 and you have a bank loan on it for $40,000, you have an asset worth $60,000. The opposite of an asset is a liability. Tracking assets and liabilities is the way a business keeps score, and steadily increasing assets is the way it succeeds financially for the long term.

A liability is an obligation to pay a debt, for an auto loan, with a supplier, or to a bank, for example. Liabilities are acquired by contracting for services, taking out loans, financing equipment, or buying property. A steady increase in liabilities is the way builders drown in debt.

A liquid asset is cash or items that may quickly be turned into cash. Savings and checking accounts are the most liquid. Bonds and stocks must be sold, but generally this can be done within a few hours or days; thus, they are also liquid. A house, land, and long-term maturity bonds are not liquid assets because it takes months or years to convert them into cash.

Cash flow is the movement of money in and out of a business. Income brings it in; payments send it out. Negative cash flow means you can't pay the current bills without using capital or a line of credit. Positive cash flow means that you can. Managing cash flow means balancing the incoming and the outgoing monies. A positive cash flow does not necessarily mean you are making a profit because it is possible to have lots of cash coming in while spending still more. There are various strategies to manage cash flow; learn what they are and use them.[177]

Capital, as distinct from cash flow, is the assets available to invest in the company. Capital is used to establish the business, improve it, expand it, or cover cash flow shortages. Spending company capital should provide long-term benefits, such as reducing overhead or increasing profit. Under-capitalized startups fail often and quickly, and even companies that are profitable can fail if they don't have enough capital to sustain themselves when work slows or payments are delayed.

A line of credit is a prearranged short-term loan from a lender that is available immediately in any amount up to the established limit (from thousands to millions, depending on one's financial health) for a period of a few weeks to a few months. It is used when cash flow or capital is in short supply and for unplanned expenses, such as a slow-paying customer or an unexpectedly large tax bill. A line of credit is usually approved for periods of six to twelve months and automatically renewed if it is managed well. If it is managed badly—that is, if it is used as a permanent loan instead of a short-term bridge loan—it may indicate to the lender that the business is not being managed well and the line of credit

177 See HomeTech Publishing's website under "Articles/Estimating." *The Journal of Light Construction* has several related articles on cash flow and *Consumer Reports* has valuable financial information.

may be cancelled, at which point the outstanding balance becomes due and payable immediately or converted into a long-term loan, if the lender is willing.

Cash reserve account or operating capital reserve is money incrementally deposited in a stand-alone savings account. The funds for this account come from a percentage added to the company's standard overhead figure (from 1% to 5%), and each time a payment is received that percentage is deposited into the account. The goal is to have enough to cover eight to twelve months of overhead expenses should they be required; but there is no reason to stop there. The reserve could eventually replace the need for a line of credit. It should be used only for emergencies, as a short-term line of credit, or when it gets big enough to invest in the company. *Establishing and consistently funding a cash reserve account is one of the smartest financial moves that you will ever make.*[178]

Gross, all inclusive, all things: gross revenue, gross income, gross profit.

Net, what is left after expenses have been paid: net cost, net income, net profit.

Petty cash is paper money kept on hand for small purchases. For a tradesman or a builder, it might be $500 to $1000. At times, petty cash will be used to pay vendors and small subs or to cover odds-and-ends. But track it precisely because the potential for significant sums of money evaporating is high. Everyone who uses petty cash—including the owner—must turn in receipts or pay for the item personally.

---

178 See "Strictly Business, Setting Up an OCRA," Michael Stone, *The Journal of Light Construction,* January 2003.

Job expense or direct cost is every cost directly related to the construction of a project: lumber, labor, excavation, and nails, for example. A bathtub is a job cost; office stationery is overhead. It is not as clear when deciding if job signage or what portion of the owner's time is a job cost verses overhead, but each company makes its own determination. A key point is that each expense must be charged to the same account category, every time. Established rules of accounting and your bookkeeper will help in deciding the most logical category for each item.

Overhead or fixed cost, stated as a percentage of annual gross sales, is the cost of doing business.[179] It is those items not tied directly to a job: vehicles, fuel, office staff, professional fees, advertising, and some taxes, for example. Everything not covered in job costs is overhead. Overhead is a consistent cost regardless of how many jobs are running—although it will fluctuate somewhat based on volume—and it is a hard cost that must be included in every estimate. Overhead varies significantly for a renovator, a handyman, and new home builder; because of volume and efficiency; from urban to suburban to metropolitan areas; and from one builder to the next. Therefore, each company must determine its own overhead percentage from actual costs, and it must be kept current because it changes with time and circumstances. Controlling overhead must be a priority because there is an unrelenting pressure to increase it and a built-in tendency to allow it to grow, especially when business is good.[180] Overhead is surprisingly high for small business, and not charging enough for it is a chronic problem for many new builders.

179 For example, a 33% Overhead figure for $250,000 in sales means that $82,500 is required to cover overhead. ($250,000 × 33% = $82,500)

180 See http://www.markupandprofit.com/. Also, HomeTech Publishing's website under "Articles/Estimating." For an unconventional way of charging overhead, see "How to Charge for Overhead" by Les Deal, *The Journal of Light Construction,* September 2002.

Budget is 1) an estimate—we expect to gross $250,000 this year—or a goal—to do $250,000 we must generate $21,000 in sales per month; 2) a sum of money allowed for a specific purpose for a fix period of time—$3000 may be spent on computer software this year. Developing a budget for the entire company from scratch can be overwhelming. Instead, start small, ask the bookkeeper or accountant for help, and slowly widen the use of budgets over time.

Profit or net profit is what is left after job costs and overhead are paid. It is the reward for the company's skill, effort, and risk. There are complex formulas and definitions describing profit. What ultimately matters is that at the end of each job, there is free cash to bank. If you don't make a profit, the business—your hopes and dreams—cannot work. That is not to say that profit is the only thing that matters— it isn't—but if the business does not consistently make a profit, it will go out of business or worse, struggle for years barely surviving.

Break-even point is the point at which the job and overhead costs are covered, everything above that point is profit.

"…if one advances confidently in the direction
of his dreams, and endeavors to live the life
which he has imagined, he will meet with a
success unexpected in common hours."
—Henry David Thoreau

MONEY NOTES

Principles

Learning to manage money becomes easier with practice. It may be difficult at first, but it will be life changing when you learn to do it well.

> "There are plenty of ways to get ahead. The first is so basic I'm almost embarrassed to say it: spend less than you earn." —Paul Clitheroe

———————

Measuring one's happiness in dollars is a grave mistake. It appears to be human nature to believe that if a salary of $50,000 a year is good than $100,000 is better and $150,000 better still. Having enough money to live well is important. But objects are only part of what creates a worthwhile life; family, friends, learning, growing, volunteering, and using your creative abilities are far more important.

> "Anybody who thinks money will make you happy, hasn't got money." —David Geffen

———————

Value is based on perception. We will happily pay for an object one day that a week before we believed to be outrageously overpriced. The value of a thing—from a diamond-tipped drill bit to 100 acres of land—is based on the degree to which we believe it will allow us to accomplish a goal, meet a need, or provide for future success.

> "He is rich according to what he is, not according to what he has." —H. W. Beecher

———————

Be financially frugal. Pay your bills on time. Build assets.

———————

Every one of the established companies from whom you buy includes overhead and profit in what they sell. The ones that didn't are no longer in business.

———————

Residential construction companies can expect between 10% and 25% profit based on gross income. In a high-volume business, it may be as low as 5%, while a company with an appealing product in a hot market may make 50% for a time. Construction is a tough business and the reward for doing it well should be *at least* a 15% to 20% profit. The percentage of profit earned will vary by the strength of the sales force, accuracy of estimates, competency of field staff, quality of fiscal controls, type of business, and the state of the local and national economies.

———————

Build your credit rating and protect it carefully.

———————

It is okay to have money sit in the bank. Although it is tempting, you do not need to increase your salary, buy new equipment, or renovate the offices when you have extra money, even a lot of extra money.

> "If you would be wealthy, think of saving as well as getting." —Benjamin Franklin

———————

A business slowdown is not always a bad thing. If your finances are in order—bills current, low overhead, few liabilities, and money in the bank—a slowdown could allow for reorganizing and refining the business, letting go of marginal employees, and perhaps taking a vacation.

———————

Strategies

Your goal is not to be inexpensive. Instead, work to provide the intangibles that make a construction company stand out—organization, quality, service—and for which clients will pay. In construction, the guy focusing on low price is the one who goes out of business quickly or, perhaps even worse, struggle endlessly to stay afloat.

Capital for a new business may come from the owner, be borrowed from a lender, or supplied by an investor.[181] The capital required is dependent on the type and size of the business and how soon it will begin to generate income. To estimate the capital required, create a comprehensive list (a budget) of the startup costs—office space and equipment, accountant-lawyer, sales-marketing, taxes-payroll[182]—and estimate the cost for monthly overhead and include a contingency. Ideally have enough capital to cover the initial startup costs plus six to twelve months of overhead expenses.[183]

> "Well, I think that there's a very thin dividing line
> between success and failure. And I think if you
> start a business without financial backing, you're
> likely to go the wrong side of that dividing line."
> —Richard Branson

---

181 If possible, begin with your own money. Interest payments increase overhead and lessen cash flow. Sharing profit with an investor can be expensive and frustrating.

182 The U.S. Small Business Administration (SBA) and SCORE Associates have information on their websites to help in determining the costs involved in starting a business.

183 This target is worth shooting for, but many successful companies have started with less. That said, not having enough capital will make life considerably harder and the company's survival more tenuous.

Use earnings—profit—not dollar volume to measure the health of your company. With a good profit margin in the right trade, it is possible to make a comfortable living grossing $200,000 a year. It is also possible to gross $3,000,000 and struggle mightily if there is little or no profit.

The owner's salary does not come out of profit. It comes out of job-cost if they work in the field, overhead if they work in the office, or a percentage from each if they split their time.

Strategies to improve cash flow:

- Make the first draw large and the rest small and frequent.

- Make the last draw 80% of the remaining balance at "substantial completion" with what remains due upon completion.

- Pay employees every two weeks.

- Require draws as a phase begins not when it is complete.

- Meet with a slow-paying client immediately to find out why and solve the problem.

- Use credit cards. (But *never pay interest on credit card debt*.)

- Establish and use trade charge accounts.

- Have assets or a line of credit available for shortfalls.

Trust your accounting system to determine the cost of overhead. New builders often don't believe that overhead could be as high as it is and some reduce the figure in their estimates. But if your accounting system is accurate, that is your true cost of overhead, and either the customer will pay it or the company will. In residential construction—depending on many factors such as size, location, or type of work, for example—overhead will run from 20% to 50% of gross sales.

———————

Review overhead costs often and tightly control them. If you don't, one day they will grow large enough to dictate job selection and business decisions. Or they might put your out of business.

———————

Differentiate between essential and nonessential expenses. For one month, keep a precise list of what you personally spend money on for the business. It is annoying, but do it anyway. Then divide the list into essentials and nonessentials and multiply the nonessentials by twelve months. Catch your breath. You must spend money to operate a business, but distinguishing between the important and the unimportant is vital because it is possible to spend an astonishing amount of money on junk, whims, and nonsense.

> "Beware of little expenses. A small leak will sink a great ship." —Benjamin Franklin

———————

Do not buy large items on impulse. Discuss it with those involved to decide if a real need exists and if the business can afford it. And wait a few days. With time, what seemed essential often becomes unnecessary or a better solution is found. If you decide that the item will add real value, buy it, but only after thoroughly researching prices and options.[184]

Bankruptcy, if it becomes necessary, is not the end of the world. I am not advocating it. If possible it should be avoided. But if it is inevitable, there are worse things. Scores of famous people have declared bankruptcy—U.S. presidents (Grant and Lincoln), founders of major U.S. corporations (Disney, Hershey, Ford), countless builders, and actors/musicians in droves—many of whom went on to great success.

> "The greatest glory in living lies not in never
> falling, but in rising every time we fall."
> —Nelson Mandela

Money and Jobs

Remain frugal from startup through completion on every job. It is generally when all is going well that we decide that there is "plenty of money" in a job and start spending freely. But expenses have a way of expanding toward the end of a project to take up every available dollar and more.

Profit is an ambition until each job is complete. New builders sometimes believe that the money collected from jobs is theirs to spend, but there is no faster way to get into trouble in contracting.

---

184 *Consumer Reports* is a great place to begin your research if it covers the item you are interested in buying.

You cannot depend on a property going to closing even when you have a sales contract in hand. Closings fall through for countless reasons, often at the last possible minute and often when you have been given the most adamant assurances that the property will close. This is a difficult situation because once a property is under contract you want to move on to the next project, but if you extend yourself based on anticipated income and it falls through, it could cripple the business.

Don't be shy about billing and collecting money. If you have fulfilled the contract terms, expect payment on time and in full. Place an initial line everywhere payment is mentioned in the contract and, during the contract signing, review those sections with the client and have them initial each one. When a payment is on time, let them know you appreciate it. The first time a payment is late, discuss the terms again and make it clear that late payment is unacceptable. Explain that if you are not paid on time and in full, you will exercise your option of slowing down or pulling off the job.[185] Be prepared for the commotion this may cause, but do not shy away from it. If you have done the work as agreed, it is your money and you have every right to get it—now. Always be professional and use common sense. Do not cause a problem where none exists.

Expenses continue even when a job is complete. A bill may arrive late or warranty work may be required. Therefore, do not close job files out for three to six months or more after completion and set money aside to cover the unexpected.

---

185 There are other options such as putting a lien on the property or suing, but do not even allude to them until you have tried every reasonable alternative, consulted with an attorney, and decided there is no other option. If it comes to that, it will be expensive and messy and usually the process will benefit no one but the lawyers.

You are not a lender; do not finance clients' work. Avoid easy payment terms or being too patient when an invoice is overdue.

––––––––––

Avoid moving money between jobs. By starting several new jobs, jumping around between them, and shuffling money— that is, using draws from one job to pay expenses on others— you can run a company for a year or more while losing money the entire time and suddenly—although not really if you are paying attention—find yourself out of business.

––––––––––

You are not responsible for clients' money problems. Toward the end of a job, clients may realize they misjudged their finances, spent more than intended, or feel buyers' remorse. Having sympathy for their position is fine, but do not take it on by working for free or waiting to get paid. Your responsibility is building well; theirs is paying for the work on time and in full.

––––––––––

TERMS & DEFINITIONS

This section provides an overview of key construction terms and definitions. It does not include every term or definition, and some terms are used differently based on who develops the job documents, the size of job, and the area of the country. For example, a *contract* is a contract until it morphs into a *general agreement* and the terms *scope-of-work* and *specifications* are often used interchangeably. New and smaller companies tend toward less standardized terms, but even the biggest organizations don't always agree on when or how a term is used.

Addendum (Addenda) is a supplement, revision, or clarification to the construction documents developed and published by the designer or engineer. Addenda are issued during the bidding process or when the job is underway. They are distinguished from change orders in that they do not refer to time or cost and clients do not generally sign off on them. Addenda issued during the bidding process must be read carefully because they provide the answers to questions put to the designer by every contractor developing a bid for that job.

Allowance, a dollar amount budgeted in an estimate for each item that has not been chosen, designed, or specified at the time the estimate is being prepared.[186] Allowances are required because a job is being fast-tracked, some bit of information cannot be known (what is underground for example), or an item has not been selected for various reasons. Allowances let a job move forward without requiring every decision to be made but still provide a complete list of what is included and an approximate cost on the allowance items, thus making a complete estimate possible.

---

186 For example, if $600 is allowed for a dishwasher, when the item is selected by the client and purchased by the builder, the amount over or under $600 is charged or credited to the client in the next billing cycle or change order.

Allowance Notes

When pricing allowances, include enough money to cover all of the costs: finding, ordering, estimating, picking up, shipping, breakage, supervision, tests, inspections, permits, and O&P, either in the allowance figure or in the base estimate, depending on the type of allowance used.

———

There are four types of allowances: labor-only, material-only, labor & material, and complete. With the first three, only the cost for the named item—labor or material—is adjusted when an allowance is used, while all of the other costs—supervision, inspection, certification, insurance, bonds, permits, testing, and overhead & profit (O&P)—are included in the base estimate and they do not change. The problem with the first three methods is that, if the client chooses an especially complex or exotic item, the builder is unable to charge for the added liability, expense, effort, and O&P. With the forth type, the complete allowance, regardless of what is chosen the builder is paid for his added costs and, if the client remains at or near the allowance amount and the item is not overly complex, there is no added cost. Some contracts stipulate that a labor-only or material-only allowance must be used. In that case, add significant contingencies to the cost of the allowance.

———

Too many allowances on a project indicate the client can't make decisions or the designer is not doing the work required. In either case, if something does not change, there will be serious problems as the job proceeds.

———

Some contracts require the builder to pass along trade discounts to the client on allowance items. This is ridiculous. Unless you are doing this on the entire project—that is, reselling everything to the client at cost—there is no reason to do it with allowances, and that is doubly so if you are tied to a material-only or labor-only allowance or you won the work through a competitive bid.

———————

There are downsides to using allowances: Decisions put off to the last minute disrupt the construction schedule, too many allowances inevitably cause problems, and, if clients consistently exceed the allowance amounts, it will often cause friction between them and whoever priced the allowances. To lessen these issues: push to get as many decisions as possible before starting,[187] provide a comprehensive list of allowances in the contract including a date by which each item must be chosen and a charge if a nondecision disrupts construction, and, each time an item exceeds the allowance amount, let clients know how their choice affects the cost and the schedule. Document these discussions.

———————

Never guess or ballpark the cost of an allowance.

———————

Allowance costs are given in units: lump-sum, linear foot, square foot, square yard, per square (roofing), cubic yard (excavation), or each.

———————

187 Some companies will not begin work until every item is selected and every issue resolved, and some require that all of the materials are in stock locally or in their own warehouse before beginning work. Either practice eliminates the need for most allowances.

On larger projects, the people making the allowance selection—usually the client or designer—are responsible for providing product details: manufacturer's name, model number, color, texture, size, drawings, specs, and other information as required. If a selection is exotic or difficult to find, they should also tell you where to find the item. If you are required to do this work, be certain to include the additional cost in the allowance figure because it can be time consuming.

There may be any number of allowances on a project, but each one should be written out separately—that is, not lumped together with others—so that they are easier to track and invoice.

At the contract signing, explain to the client what an allowance is: how it is billed, how their allowance choices affect the construction schedule and the total cost of the job.

Allowances are most often required for finished items. For items such as light and plumbing fixtures, paint colors, and floor coverings, decisions can reasonably be put off until later in the job, allowing clients to see the finished space before making their selections.

If the contractor orders the wrong item or the owners or designers change their mind once an item is ordered, the party responsible for the mistake or the change pays the re-stocking fee and associated costs.

The contractor is responsible for breakage once the item is on-site. Before that, the supplier is.

When estimating an allowance, provide the most accurate figure you can. Match the selection to the project's overall quality level, and never low-ball numbers to make the price more appealing. If you do, once the job is underway and the allowances are coming in higher than priced, you will appear incompetent or dishonest, and it will cause hard feelings and mistrust.

When clients exceed an allowance by a small amount, let it go. Don't nickel and dime them.

Alternates and variations on alternates are prices provided by the bidder to do part of the work differently then detailed in the job documents. For example, if the construction documents call for a carport, the alternate might be to build a garage instead, while a variation on the alternate might be a 16' garage door instead of two 8' doors. While the cost of the carport is included in the base bid, the alternates and variations on alternates are separate cost items, which the client has the option of selecting. Alternates work, although like allowances, there are potential problems: the likelihood of error increases as their number and variations grow; when getting free bids, including a few simple well-defined alternates may not be unreasonable but including many complex ones is; the details on alternates are often incomplete, making accurate pricing difficult or impossible; builders sometimes assume alternates will not be selected and guesstimate a price only to have the alternate chosen and find that their price is far to low.[188]

188 Instead of asking for free bids and then piling on alternates, which is entirely unreasonable, the client or designer should pay someone to provide pricing during the design process so that the client can make informed choices before the job is put out to bid. This would eliminate the need for alternates. Or, after the contract is awarded, the winning bidder should be asked to price the alternates.

Back charging is the act of billing someone or withholding money from a payment—from a sub or a supplier, for example—when they have not fulfilled part of the contract terms or if they have caused damage to the job. Back charges usually cause intense anger and sometimes retaliation. So before using it, talk with the party and, if possible, allow them to correct the issue. If they are clearly responsible and they can't or won't correct the problem, back charging is reasonable.

Bond, a legal agreement to pay monies if specific acts are not satisfied by the individual or company buying the bond. For example, if a builder buys a performance bond and signs a contract to build a project but does not complete it for any reason, the company issuing the bond pays to have the project completed. Bonds are a form of insurance for the client and they are typically sold by banks and insurance companies. Bonds are common on large commercial projects and government work at all levels, but extremely rare in small commercial and residential construction, although municipalities and state highway departments may require a bond for cutting a street to install a water line, for example.

- **Bid bond** pays in those cases where the GC has provided a bid but refuses to contract to do the work.

- **Performance or completion bond** pays in those cases where the work has begun but the contractor defaults and does not complete the project.

- **Payment bond** pays when the GC does not pay his subs or suppliers on a bonded project.

Change orders (CO) [189] detail and record job modifications made during construction, and they legally alter the construction contract when signed by the parties involved. Besides detailing additions and changes to the work, they give the cost or credit involved and note the old and the

189 See Sample, Change Order in the Appendix.

new contract price, the cumulative cost of change orders issued to date, changes to the schedule, and the terms of payment. A CO may list one or several changes on a single document and any number of COs may be issued during a project. COs are written, submitted, and tracked by the GC or sub.[190] As explained in the CO Notes below, COs are more often required on fixed-price contracts than cost-plus or T&M contracts. However, COs must be a standard part of your paperwork system and ready to be used on any type of contract as required.

Change Order Notes

Include a sample change order with each proposal or bid submitted. Explain what it is, the terms of payment, and when COs will be used:

- When a client adds or changes something or makes a decision that was put off.

- When a designer or engineer requires changes or revisions.

- When an unknowable or undefined item requires an addition or a change.

- When a government agency requires something extra or unexpected.

- When money for an allowance is spent.[191]

---

190 Some contracts (AIA for example) call for the designer to issue COs, but I have seen very few CO's issued by designers. In residential work, it is rare, partly because clients are often unwilling to pay the designer to create and administer COs, but mostly because it is more practical for the GC to estimate and schedule the work after sorting out the details with the client, the designer, and the trade. Even if the designer develops drawings and specs for the change, the GC must estimate and arrange for the work and therefore in most cases, it still makes more sense for him to issue and track COs.

191 Some companies make financial adjustments for allowances in their draw schedule, not through change orders.

New builders often avoid using COs. They imagine themselves to be generous, or they believe there is "plenty of money" in the contract, or they are trying to avoid causing friction. What often happens is that as the project is winding down, they realize they are losing money, and they scramble to create COs to recover their losses. This almost never works, and, regardless of the outcome, it will cause intense friction. Use COs early and as often as necessary.

―――――

If you don't use COs early in the construction process, clients will reasonably assume that everything is included in the contract price and they will resist their use later on.

―――――

Conflicts are inevitable if COs are not used on fixed-price contracts. COs require issues to be defined and resolved, details documented, and clients to sign-off on the changes and the cost. Therefore, even when there is a credit, no cost is involved, or you agree to pay for the change, write a CO.

―――――

All change orders cost the builder money. Even those for which the client receives a credit or there is no charge, because they require discussion, estimating, schedule changes, and material handling. Therefore, include these costs—or deduct them from a CO credit—when writing a CO. The amount charged must be determined on a case-by-case basis since the circumstances vary widely, but always be fair to both the client and the company.

―――――

Cost-plus (CP) and time & material (T&M) contracts lessen the need for COs and the administrative and billing process they require. On large projects, changes can number in the hundreds and having to detail, estimate, and write a CO for each one and then relay that information to the field is time consuming and expensive. Working with a CP or T&M contract allows many of the changes to be worked out on the spot with the foreman or tradesman, estimated, and implemented immediately, causing significantly fewer delays and lower cost. However, using these contracts does not eliminate the need to document changes. It may be less formal than a CO, but there must an official list of the changes, with the client signing off on them. For contentious, complex, or expensive changes, use a CO.

It is common for a client to insist that some change be done right away, in the excitement of the moment, whatever the cost. But when they see the bill, they balk at the price and claim they were misunderstood. Yet another reason to maintain a strict policy of creating and receiving approval for every CO before work begins.

When adding one bit of work and removing another, you and the client might decide to swap one for the other and not bother to write a CO. But writing COs requires discussion, reflection, and documentation, thus providing an opportunity—or an excuse, if required—to think through what the change actually requires and the costs involved.

There are various ways to collect for change orders: add the cost to the contract price and get paid by the draw schedule, get paid when the work is complete, charge a percentage up front with the balance paid when the work is done, or collect payment in full at the time the CO is signed by the client. The last method is best because work on COs is generally done immediately, it cuts down on paperwork, and it adds to the company's cash flow.

———————

According to some contracts, if you wait beyond a specific time frame to submit a change order you lose the right to charge for that item.

———————

Completion and substantial completion. *Completion* is defined as a project being done entirely with not a single thing remaining. *Substantial completion* is the point at which a space becomes available to be used as intended with a few minor items to be completed. A kitchen that is waiting for a backsplash to be installed but which can be used in the mean time is an example of a substantially completed project. While completion is straightforward, substantial completion—and the payment that comes with it—is open to interpretation and, therefore, often disagreement.

Contingency is money or time added to cover for uncertainty or an emergency. For example, extra money is added to an estimate because the specs are vague or extra weeks are added to a construction schedule to account for the rainy season. Contingencies are important when providing a bid because no estimator can know everything that will happen. Therefore when bidding competitively, a 10% to 30% contingency—or more depending on the circumstances and the quality of the job documents—might be added to cover the unknown.

Construction cost database or estimating database is a collection of itemized construction tasks and their costs—known as "line items"—arranged according to a construction index.[192]

Construction documents or job documents may consist of one page or a hundred pages, but regardless of size, their purpose is to define and detail a project so that the legal terms and conditions may be agreed to and the project built to meet the clients' needs. Each set of construction documents provides basic information: names, contact information, job location, scope-of-work, specifications, cost, payment terms, schedule, and warranty details. For small jobs, a tradesman develops specs and a price and provides a simple contract including the basic information and perhaps a cut sheet or a simple drawing. On midsized jobs, a large trade or GC provides the basics while adding schematics, engineering calculations, and more detailed drawings and general conditions. On large projects, either a design-build firm develops a full-blown set of job documents or an independent design firm creates plans and specifications and the GC incorporates these into the contract by reference. Although formats and standards do exist, all contracts—even those written by the same author—are specifically and often structurally different than their predecessor. And construction documents change as a project proceeds through the use of addenda and change orders as choices are made, changes requested, problems arise, and solutions found.

Contract is a signed document, enforceable by law, between named parties—owner–builder, builder–sub—creating obligations and detailing the rights, responsibilities, and relationship of the parties. The word *contract* is sometimes used more broadly to include all job documents.

---

192 See Sample, Construction Index in the Appendix; note the line item costs in the center columns.

Contract Notes

Collect and study contracts. Begin now and continue until you have a clear understanding of the forms, concepts, and issues they address. The sooner you acquire a working knowledge of contract language, the sooner it will become an established part of your business routine.[193]

———————

Read and understand the meaning and the consequences of every clause in every contract before you sign. It is time-consuming and the need for it never ends, but as you become familiar with contract language, it will get easier. When starting out, use a legal dictionary and ask your lawyer or a knowledgeable friend for help with those items that you do not understand.

———————

Use a contract on every job and for every relationship: GC–client–sub–professional. When starting out, use a standard preprinted form. As your knowledge and experience grow, create documents to fit your situation and need.

———————

Use clear concise contracts that use plain English. Some contracts are unbearably long and dense while others are clear and brief but still include all of the necessary details. Rule of thumb: if it is not fairly easy for you to understand, no one else will understand it either.

———————

193 Where to find contracts: National Association of Home Builders (NAHB), New England Business Service (NEBS), books, trade magazines, the web, and friends in the trades. Also, see the Appendix for a few sample contracts.

Do not have your lawyer write your contracts. It is too expensive and some lawyers will complicate it beyond reason or need. Contracts already exist that can be revised or used as is. And, most importantly, researching and writing them yourself will require you to be knowledgeable about their content and involved in their evolution. When starting out, consider having your lawyer review completed contracts.

———————

No contract is perfect, therefore, never stop refining or replacing them as the company grows and changes.

———————

Do not use an extremely long, small-print contract. Many clients and subs will refuse to sign it and, at some point, a too-complex contract becomes meaningless.

———————

Keep your contracts as word processing files. This provides the flexibility to meet the specific needs of each job, and it allows clauses to be saved, added, and revised easily.

———————

When writing contracts, list every job-related document: blueprint, spec, permit, agreement, schematic, structural drawing, and addendum, for example. Include title, date, author, and other identifying characteristics, making them and the information they contain legally part of the project.

———————

Place financial responsibility for the poorly defined or unknowable with the client. This includes what's under the ground, poor plans or specs, or what government agencies require in special situations, for example.

_____

There will be times you choose not to get everything into a contract or a change order. You might even decide not to use them at all, because you know the client or it is a small job and believe that it will be okay, which it will be—until it isn't. Unfortunately, this is a lesson that many of us learn over, and over, and over again.

> "Put it in writing. If it is not written down, it never happened." —Tom King

_____

Before clients sign a contract, review it with them. Explain key points—payment schedule and start and finish dates, for example—and anything that they are unclear about. It is important that clients know what they are agreeing to, and later, if there are problems, they cannot claim they did not understand what they were signing.

_____

You can handwrite revisions in the margin of a contract. Although not ideal, those notes are legally binding as long as they are legible, the meaning is clear, the same note is written on each signed copy, and each note is initialed by the same people who signed the original contract.

_____

Some contracts include penalties for late completion. Monetary penalties, also called liquidated damages, assess a penalty for each day a project runs past an agreed-upon completion date. Such penalties are rare in residential work but not unheard of. Many builders will not agree to them, especially if the project was won through a competitive bid because the margins are so tight. If you do agree to a penalty clause, be certain that the completion date is extended for every day lost on items over which you have no control—weather, building regulations, change orders, plan revisions—and that a bonus be paid for each day that the job is completed ahead of schedule. Also, include contractual terms requiring subs to pay a penalty if they delay completion, but do not agree to pay a bonus if they complete early because their completion dates have more flexibility than the GCs.[194]

———————

"Right of rescission" gives clients the right to rescind or cancel a contract without penalty within three business days of signing.[195] It is a required contract clause in some states. The intent is to give clients who have been pressured into signing a contract time to reconsider and cancel it without cost or penalty.

———————

The best contracts fairly balance the risk between clients and builders. If they don't, if the builder accepts most or all of the risk, he must include significant contingencies to cover the unknown and greater profit to reward him for assuming that risk.

———————

[194] See *The Journal of Light Construction,* "Guarantee Your Completion Dates," by Paul Eldrenkamp for an interesting take on liquidated damages.

[195] The time period varies by state.

Avoid contracts that dictate how much overhead and profit the contractor can charge. If you find one, run the other way. Overhead is nonnegotiable and a 10% profit does not justify the company assuming the risk or using their knowledge and resources. Most builders who agree to these contacts, add their additional O&P to the line item costs or recover it through change orders, and those that don't go out of business while the job is underway or soon after.

———————

Most subs write a contract to cover their work. You will need to review and sign it, but develop an addendum to add to their contract covering items that you need to be included.[196]

———————

Adhere tightly to the terms of your own contact. If you don't, it will cause problems with the client, and if a dispute ends up in court or arbitration, the fact that you ignored your own contract will look bad. If you cannot or choose not to meet certain terms of your contract, revise or remove them in future contracts.

———————

Construction index is a classification system used to organize construction data, including specifications, estimates, and schedules. Indexes are arranged sequentially by number, in the order that the work is preformed, and divided into headings, sub-headings, and line items.[197] The Uniform Construction Index (UCI) is the closest thing to a residential index that I'm aware of, and many residential builders and

---

196 See Sample, Subcontractor Agreement in the Appendix.

197 See Sample, Construction Index in the Appendix; note the major headings, sub-headings, and line items.

the software programs designed for them use the original UCI or a modified version of it.[198]

Construction schedule (CS) is a list of tasks required to build a project, arranged according to a timeline. In its simplest form, it consists of notes on a pad, while more complex schedules include start and finish dates, resources (labor, subs, equipment), dependencies (which item must be completed before another starts), and other information. The most common forms of CSs, in order of usefulness: pad and paper, a white board, a listing in Excel, bar charts, and the Critical Path Method (CPM).[199]

Scheduling Notes

Scheduling software programs handle huge amounts of information. The programs allow schedules to be reorganized quickly and referred to and shared easily. The information can be presented in written or graphic form, making it easier to understand and use.

———————

Start using scheduling software early in your career. Teach yourself or take a class, but begin early and increase the complexity as your skills increase.

———————

198 Several years ago the UCI evolved into MasterFormat, which currently has about fifty divisions and nearly 7500 line items (2013) with its primary focus on large-scale construction. I believe that the index is far too complex and the estimating and spec-writing programs based on it far too expensive for most residential builders. Construction Specifications Institute (CSI) claims to hold the copyright for the original UCI but no longer promotes or supports the product—they threatened a lawsuit if I included a copy in this book—but there are many versions of the UCI available online and in estimating programs.

199 Microsoft Project, standard or professional versions, is more complex and expensive than some scheduling programs but it is easy to learn, flexible, and compatible with other Microsoft products; it can be used collaboratively; and you will never out grow it.

While in theory every conceivable item can be listed in a CS, too much information makes creating, maintaining, and using it cumbersome.

Most CS software provides templates, task lists, and examples.

A CS is an estimate of time. Exactly like a cost estimate, it involves items over which you exert fairly reliable control—employees, delivery dates, good subs—and those over which you exert little or no control—weather, bad subs, clients, designers, government authorities—and, thus, the most useful schedules remain as animated and pliable as the construction process itself.

Remind people that a construction schedule is an estimate, not a guarantee. When sharing a CS with customers, subs, designers, or suppliers, inform them that the schedule is a forecast, that it will change, and that it comes with no implied guarantees. Write this in capital letters at the bottom of the schedule and note it in contracts.

The line items from an estimate can usually be used as an outline for the construction schedule.

A well-done schedule is an indispensable tool. Developing a schedule—breaking out tasks, arranging them, working out dependencies, assigning time and resources—requires one to think through the process, to get others' input, to list what is known, and to get answers to what is unknown.

CSs are created for each job. A master schedule provides an overview of all jobs underway or coming up. This helps to coordinate dates and resources.

———————

On larger jobs, involve key people in creating the schedule. One person should rough it out and then major contributors—manager, lead carpenter, major subs—should meet to make it as accurate as possible and also to get each of them to buy-into the timeline.

———————

A thorough and accurate CS is a powerful sales tool.

———————

An accurate CS helps subs plan their work. This allows for fewer excuses, and over time it will help to attract and keep the best subs.

———————

Draw schedule or payment schedule is included in the contract to spell out how and when the contractor is to be paid and how nonstandard items—special orders, allowances, and change orders, for example—are handled. Most draw schedules begin with a down payment before starting work, provide for progress payments based on a time period—every two weeks, for example—or at the beginning or end of construction phases—excavation, framing, and so on—and detail when the substantial and final payments are due. There is no perfect draw schedule. On larger jobs, their terms are usually negotiated. The good ones are easily understood, implemented, and fair to all parties, providing financial protection to the client and cash flow to the contractor.[200] Be rigidly honest when billing, openly discuss delays and

200 If a draw schedule has been used repeatedly but a client insists on revising it significantly, warning bells should go off. Negotiate with care, be certain that the terms provide for adequate cash flow and that the draws are based on reasonable factors.

problems, don't bill for unfinished items, let the client know when an invoice is coming, and resolve every billing issue immediately.

General conditions, also called contract terms or general agreements, detail the terms and conditions under which a project is to be built. Each company uses a different format for its contract terms—or calls them by a different name—and, of course, the details change somewhat on each project.[201]

General conditions, special or supplemental, detail the local and specific project conditions and are used to amend or extend the general conditions in an AIA Contract. They are not typically used in residential work unless it is a very large project.

Labor burden is the cost a company pays for an employee on top of their salary or hourly pay rate. It is the taxes and fees that are mandated by law and the benefits the company chooses to pay. It includes payroll taxes, workers' compensation insurance, health care, sick days, training, retirement programs, insurance, and various other items. The actual figure varies significantly—typically from 25% to 50% and even higher for unions—by trade, state, benefits provided, and other factors. For example, a 50% labor burden for a $25-per-hour carpenter will add $12.50 to his labor rate. That is, the GC must charge the client $37.50 per hour ($25 + 12.50) for that employee before adding O&P. The labor burden will be different for each employee, and it will change over time, almost always moving higher. Labor burden is distinct from overhead; however, there is some discretion as to which items are included in which category. For example,

---

201 Also see AIA document A201-2007, "General Conditions of the Contract for Construction," for the longest and most detailed general conditions of which I am aware.

some people include a foreman's truck and cell phone in the labor burden while others include them in the overhead.

Lawsuit, Mediation, and Arbitration:

Lawsuit is the process of suing or being sued in a court of law, as opposed to using mediation or arbitration.

Mediation is a nonbinding[202] negotiation between parties— suppliers–GC, sub—GC—using a neutral third party approved by the participants to resolve disputes. Mediation may be done in an informal manner, by selecting a person known and trusted by all parties, for example, or more formally by choosing someone trained in mediation.

Arbitration is a more formal manner of dispute resolution than mediation but falls short of bringing the issue to court. Arbitration is binding[203] and is carried out in a formal setting with, hopefully, an informed and impartial professional arbiter. Some contracts require the use of arbitration to settle disputes, but before agreeing to these terms, read extensively about the pros and cons of each method.[204]

Mechanic's lien and waiver of lien. A mechanic's lien is a legal action taken by a GC, sub, or material supplier against a client's property to assure that they get paid for their work. A lien is placed only if there is a problem—the client refuses to pay their bill, for example—and typically your lawyer would place a lien. A waiver of lien is a legal document signed by the GC, sub, or material supplier acknowledging that they

202 That is, if the parties fail to reach an agreement, either party may walk away from the process at any time.

203 That is, the parties agree to be legally bound by the arbiter's decision and, unlike mediation, they may not reject the decision or walk away from the process.

204 See the American Arbitration Association (AAA) for more information. *Fine Home Building* and *The Journal of Light Construction* each have articles on the subject.

have received payment, in full or in part, and therefore they legally waive the right to place a mechanic's lien on the client's property. There are different types of mechanic's liens and lien waivers; discuss the options with your lawyer.

Mobilization or job setup is the work that is done to get a site ready before construction can start: gathering and moving material and equipment on-site, setting up a shop or tool shed, or protecting sidewalks and shrubs, for example. Mobilization should be included as a distinct cost item in larger estimates.

OSHA (Occupational Safety And Health Administration) is the regulatory arm of the U.S. Department of Labor ostensibly responsible for safety on construction sites. At one time it was primarily concerned with commercial work, but in recent years it has broadened its focus and now actively regulates (some would say harasses) residential builders. In my opinion, OSHA uses its nearly dictatorial powers to achieve highly questionable results while adding significant cost to the construction process. While safety is of primary importance on every job, Lord please save us from the desk-bound bureaucrat making excessive and impractical regulations: after donning a hardhat, securing ladders, setting up railings, tying off, and dragging a rope and harness around all day long, you may wish you could fall off the one story roof and end it all. If OSHA is active your area, the best advice I can give you is to learn its rules and follow them the best that you can and add a charge to every job—call it an OSHA tax—and put the money into an account to be used to comply with OSHA regulations and pay its fines.

> "OSHA: A protective coating made by half-baking a mixture of fine print, red tape, split hairs, and bullshit—usually applied at random with a shotgun."
> —Anonymous

Plans, Drawings, or Blueprints are two-dimensional multipage scaled diagrams detailing what is to be built in either an architectural or engineering format. A set of drawings is printed on paper ranging from 8.5" × 11" to 24" × 36" and more and more often plans are available digitally.

Plan Notes

Plans are drawn to scale. That is, at ¼" scale a 12' × 16' room is reduced to 3" and 4" lines on the page. At ½" scale, the same room is represented by 6" and 8" lines.

Architectural plans include various views of the subject (elevation, plan, section, detail, perspective), symbols to depict standard items (light fixture, toilet, framing), dimensions (33' × 60'), and the relationship of parts to each other and the building to the site. Most also include electrical (layout, fixtures, audio, alarm, vacuum systems), mechanical (heating, ventilating, air conditioning [HVAC], and plumbing), landscaping, grading, and construction details (foundation, framing, finishes).

Learn how to read blueprints. Reading blueprints is a matter of understanding their organization, nomenclature, and the meaning of lines and symbols. Read books, ask someone knowledgeable to show you the basics, and, most important, spend time studying different sets of plans. Notice how different firms vary the layout, sections, specifications, details, notes, symbols, and the amount of information that is provided.

Most plans, although not all, include an index or legend explaining the meaning of the symbols used in the drawings.

———————

Engineering drawings are different from architectural drawings. They use different formats, scales, nomenclature, and symbols to display their subject. Ask an engineer to explain the basics and study a few sets of engineering blueprints.

———————

Schematics are diagrams using symbols to depict mechanical systems. These are used in plumbing, HVAC, and electrical layouts, for example. Schematic drawings are usually not drawn to scale.

———————

Shop drawings are produced by a supplier, sub, manufacturer, or fabricator. They illustrate items that are to be prefabricated or assembled on-site. Roof truss designs or kitchen cabinet layouts are examples of when a shop drawing is produced.

———————

A cut sheet or data sheet provides product information. This includes dimensions, specifications, variations, options, textures, and colors available from the manufacturer. Cut sheets are found at suppliers or online.

———————

Submittals are materials submitted to the designer, engineer, or client by the GC or sub for review and approval. Submittals can be shop drawings, schematic diagrams, cut sheets, item certifications, or material and product samples. A GC might submit siding samples for review and approval by the client or a footing design to a municipal engineer for verification and signoff.

Plan notes are the comments and instructions on blueprints providing miscellaneous information and reminders. A note might point out which bushes are to be removed or a nonstandard condition in the existing framing.

Pre-meetings:

Pre-bid meetings are scheduled by the firm designing the project in order to distribute information and answer all of the bidders' questions at once. Pre-bid meetings are also used by contractors on larger projects for subs and suppliers for the same purpose.

Preconstruction or hand-off meetings (with client) are scheduled by the GC, or occasionally the designer, and they include the client, the GC and his staff, and possibly key subs. Often the sales department "hands-off" the job to the construction department at these meetings and introduces the client to the job foreman, who takes over the meeting and asks and answers questions, explains what will happen next, communicates current information, and reviews and highlights important points in the contract or the construction schedule. Having been through the sales and planning stages of the project, clients may have unrealistic expectations of various things and this meeting is an opportunity to diplomatically temper those expectations.

Preconstruction meetings (with staff, subs, suppliers) are scheduled by the GC—on projects large enough to warrant them—just before the work begins. These meetings offer an opportunity to communicate current information, clarify misunderstandings, confirm details, set standards, review and highlight schedules, and explain site issues. In most cases, the client is not invited to these meetings.

Punch list is a list of minor touchup and repair items required to complete a job. Punch lists are developed as the project nears completion and they grow or shrink as tasks are completed and new ones added. The final punch list is usually completed after the space is occupied.

Purchase order (PO) is a paper or electronic document issued by the buyer—a GC, for example—to a supplier or sub detailing price, quantity, and specifications for the product he intends to buy.

Purchase Order Notes

Most small companies do not use a formal purchase order system. Instead, they choose to track their purchases through their normal record-keeping systems, or they use handwritten POs for specific things, for example, exotic material orders.

————

An electronic purchase order system requires a steep learning curve and extensive upkeep. These systems are usually integrated into the company's estimating and accounting systems, allowing each purchase to be tracked from issuance to use.

————

Issuing a purchase order constitutes a legal offer to buy an item. The acceptance of the PO by the seller creates a legal obligation to sell that item at the quoted price and terms.

————

Retainage—or retained funds—is a percentage, generally from 2% to 20% of the total contract amount retained or withheld from each construction draw as it is paid by the client.[205] Retainage is regularly used on government and large commercial projects to provide an incentive for the GC and subs to complete their work quickly and to protect the owner against poor workmanship, liens, liability claims, and defaults that may arise toward the end of the project. The money is held by the client after the last payment in the draw schedule is made and paid out when all liens are released and the project is completed to the owner's satisfaction. Retainage is rarely used on residential construction because it restricts the GC's cash flow, it gives the client an unfair advantage, and most residential subs and suppliers will not agree to it. A fair payment schedule takes the place of retainage and provides adequate protection to the client.

Retainage Notes

Owners sometimes use retainage and the slow payout of retainage as a way to help finance their projects.

———————

GCs sometimes hold more retainage from their subs than is being held from them and pay retainage slowly in order to help finance their work.

———————

If a client insists on holding retainage on a residential project, the amount should be limited to from 2% to 3% of the contract amount, material retainage should be excluded, all subs should be paid in full within five

---

205 For example, on a $100,000 contract with 10% retainage and draws of $10k, $20k, $30k, $30k, and $10k, the first draw will consist of a payment of $9k with the client holding $1k, the second payment will be $18k with the client holding $2k, for a total of $3k held by the client, and so on, up to and including the final payment when the client will be holding $10,000 in retainage. When the retainage will be paid to the GC is spelled out in the contract.

to fifteen days of finishing their work satisfactorily, and retainage should not be held more than fifteen to thirty days past the entire project's final completion.

On large commercial projects and especially on local, state, and federal government projects, retainage can be held for months or even years past the completion date.

Retainage is unnecessary if a GC provides a performance bond, a letter of credit, or some other financial security to the client.

I have known GCs who, when forced to use retainage on residential jobs, increase their estimate by the amount of the retainage.

Samples—or construction samples—small-scale physical models, executed on the construction site, allowing the client or designer to see the finished color and texture before work begins on that item. For example, you may be required to lay a section of brick or tile or to paint a bit of drywall the selected color.[206] Those samples you are required to provide must be listed in the job documents so that their cost can be included in the estimate.

Schedule of values divides the total contract amount into stages of work—clearing, excavation, etc.—and these are used as the basis for progress payments in AIA contracts. The schedule of values is more elaborate and demanding than the draw schedule, which is more common in residential work.

206 Be sure that the material used for the sample is taken from the same batch as the material that will be used for the bulk of the work or the finished item may vary significantly from the sample.

Scope-of-work or project scope provides a broad summary of the work with the specifications and blueprints providing the details. The terms *scope-of-work* and *specifications* are sometimes used interchangeably.[207]

Standard and specific exclusions detail those items not included in a project.

- Standard exclusions apply to every job: for example, the client provides water and electric, thus you are not required to pay for utilities.

- Specific exclusions state those items that are excluded from a job: cedar siding will be supplied and installed but not treated, for instance. Or something that might be reasonably inferred to be part of the job but is not—a deck will be power washed but the popped nails and screws will not be set, for example.

Specifications, often called **specs,** are the written requirements giving depth and detail to the materials, products, procedures, systems, and services required to build a project. If there are blueprints, the specs provide the non-visual details; if there are no blueprints, they provide what is required to complete the work. On small projects, specs are generally included in the contract. On larger ones, they are found on the blueprints or in a separate text document. Specs for residential work are produced by tradesmen, subs, builders, design-build or design firms, and engineers. Many estimating software packages include specs, although their quality varies greatly and nearly all of them will require some rewriting to fit each project.

---

207 See Sample, Small Job Contract in the Appendix to see a basic scope-of-work.

Specification Notes

Good prewritten specs for residential work are hard to find. Unless you work exclusively from documents created by others, you will need to write them or find ones to modify to meet your needs.

———————

When selecting an estimating software program that includes specs, choose one developed exclusively for residential and light commercial work.

———————

Spec writing is a technical skill. It requires clarity, precision, and thoroughness. And it's an important one because it spells out what is to be built, and, when included in the contract, the specs become legally binding.

———————

Most software programs allow specs to be modified and saved so that they can be customized to fit your company's needs.

———————

Arcat.com is a website providing specifications for manufacture's products and related information. The service is free.

———————

When writing specs for tasks that overlap—replacing shoe molding but not the baseboard or patching drywall but not painting, for example—stating what will not be done is every bit as important as stating what will be done.

———————

Wrong or incomplete specs are exasperating. If the builder knows the specs are inadequate, he must clarify them in order to estimate the work. If he doesn't know, it is costly and intensely frustrating to find out during construction.

————————

Special order items are those items that are going to take weeks or months to order and receive: imported marble, specialty ceramic tile, and custom cabinets, for example. Just before ordering the items, have the client sign off on the selection and get paid upfront because you will generally have to pay for all or most of their cost when ordering, and once they arrive—unless they are damaged or the supplier has ordered the wrong ones—they cannot be returned. When special order items are received, check immediately and thoroughly to see if there is damage and that everything—color, style, size, details—are correct. Usually, once you have picked up a special order Item you cannot return it for any reason, even if it is broken, because you might have broken it.

Utilities are businesses set up to provide essential services to the public, such as water, sewer, gas, cable, internet, or electricity. Utilities may be owned publicly or privately. In large cities and urban areas, they are huge monopolies with entrenched bureaucracies, rigid schedules, and precise requirements. In rural areas, they tend to be more flexible and accommodating. As with the building departments, the best way to work with utilities is to learn the system.

Utility lines are generally run in or along the side of streets, which are public rights-of-way, and onto private property through easements, provided to the utilities by the land developer or the property owner, or the line from the house is run to the edge of the property and hooked into the service— gas or water, for example. Water supply and sewer disposal systems are generally publicly owned. In rural areas without distribution lines, propane and heating oil are delivered by truck to tanks on the property, the water comes from a well, and the sewer goes into a septic field, both located on the property. An on-site water well and septic system are installed, maintained, and owned by the homeowner. Nearly every home in America has electrical lines going to it, and cable and internet access are handled in several ways, and how they are delivered is changing rapidly as of this writing.

Utility Notes

Electricity, telephone, and cable wires may be run overhead or underground. Some municipalities and developments require that new construction run all cables underground.

———————————

Find out from each utility where its service will enter the house. The location will affect both the distribution point inside the house and the esthetics outside. Some utilities are more flexible than others and placement is sometimes limited by factors beyond anyone's control.

———————————

Utilities will provide written instructions and directions detailing what is required to install their service.[208] Read the information carefully. Call the utility to answer any remaining questions. If helpful, ask to meet someone from the utility on-site to get job specific questions answered. You need both an overview of what the utility does, what you need to do, and who supplies the widgets that make the

---

208 It may seem that the simplest way to get this information is through the sub who will connect the service. But most subs don't have the time, knowledge, or incentive to provide a thorough picture of the process in all its permutations. Also, the process may change from city to city, neighborhood to neighborhood, and even project to project. Therefore, it is up to you to learn from each utility what its standard process is, and double check it for each new project.

connection. Ask these questions: Where will the service be terminated? At the termination, what connection will you or the sub need to provide? What is required of the sub to allow them to connect to the utility's installation—license or bond, for example? What areas tend to cause problems? What paperwork must be filled out? Where does the utility fit into the construction schedule? What will it cost?[209] How much notice do they need to do the installation?

Most utilities are regulated by public commissions. If you are having a problem with a utility, contact the local authorities to find out if they can help. But don't get your hopes up. Utility commissions tend to be more concerned with large issues rather than individual situations, and they have limited power.

Water supply and wastewater disposal can be by public water and sewer, private well and septic, or a combination of the two. In most areas where public services are available, you must hook up to those services. Visit the area sewer and water departments and ask for explanations of their procedures and systems.

Miss utility and dig permits[210] are services offered by utilities around the country to locate and mark buried lines before excavation begins. There is no cost to you for these services, but you are required by law to call them in advance of digging, three days normally, giving the location of the property and the date you intend to dig. Each utility— electric, sewer, water, cable, internet, gas—will come to your property and mark on the ground in different colored paints where its lines run. If you dig before calling them and you

---

209 As with so many things in construction, depending on the details of the project, this will be an estimate, not a fixed price, because there are variables that are impossible to predict.

210 It may be called something different in your area. Call any utility to get the contact information.

hit a cable or a gas line, you are responsible for the damage: this will delay work, it will be costly, and in extreme cases, people have been arrested for the resulting damage. If the utility marks the line incorrectly and you hit it, the utility is responsible for the cost of repairs.

—

ACKNOWLEDGEMENTS

The number of people who helped in the shaping this book over the many years it took to create, both knowingly and unknowingly, is huge: employees, clients, tradesmen, builders, family, friends, accountants, lawyers, bookkeepers, investors, inspectors, authors, manufacturers, suppliers, and many, many more. I am grateful to all of them.

Several people reviewed and commented on specific sections: Russell Poppe (lawyer), Ed Russell (building inspector), Jim Nielson (architect), Keith Kennedy (architect), Jake Covert (builder), Mike Perrone (code official), Hamid Naderi, (with ICC), Dick Morris (builder), Lee Johnson (English professor & poet), Glen Hineman (supplier), John Reynolds (designer), David Fields (accountant). Each was knowledgeable and generous with their time, and I am grateful. And there were many others: builders, tradesmen, suppliers, and designers that I interviewed over the course of thirty years whose names, regrettably, were lost in the various moves from computer to computer. I am grateful for their significant contribution, though I am unable to name them here.

Guy Maynard, the editor, was the right combination of builder, early in life, and editor for the last twenty-five years of his career. As I reviewed his edits I was aware of just how hard it must be to clarify and strengthen this nonwriters words while maintaining the intent. Thanks for taking this project on Guy. Deb Temper, of Six-Penny Graphics, was exactly the right book designer at the right time. She is creative, skilled, and patient. I'm delighted I found her. And I found Kay Cole, an indexer (right, who knew there were such people) who created two thorough indexes, making the attentive readers job easier. Lexann Henderson, my sister-in-law, donated her time and expertise to review the final text. I am grateful for the excellent work she did.

My dear friends Earl Sepella and Ezra Tishman. Earl read every word and provided advice and suggestions. Ezra found the right editor and discussed larger issues with me as they arose. But the contribution I'm most grateful for is their unwavering and enthusiastic encouragement.

And finally, and more than any other, I am profoundly grateful to my amazing wife of forty-plus years. Lisa is the reason this book exists. Besides her confidence in the idea, she read every word, sometimes several times, and made wise and invaluable suggestions. She also made it possible for me to spend the last three years completing the book and getting it published.

APPENDIX

Important: The information in this Appendix are intended to provide *basic samples* of items discussed in the text. They should not be used as legal documents. Nothing in this book is intended as legal advice. Consult an attorney with all legal questions.

"Gratitude bestows reverence, allowing us
to encounter everyday epiphanies, those
transcendent moments of awe that change
forever how we experience life and the world."
—John Milton

LISTS, FORMS, CONTRACTS, AND EXAMPLES

SAMPLE, SITE VISIT CHECK LIST

Outside building and site
- Street access: parking for workmen and unloading supplies.
- Will material need to be carried by hand to the back?
- Is there a place to store materials? Is it out of the weather?
- Is there a place to securely store tools and keep them dry?
- Does the job site need protection from theft: locks, alarms, a guard?
- Is there a place to set up and work with large tools?
- Where will the dumpster be placed?
- Is there a toilet that the workmen can use or do you need a portable toilet?[211]
- Is the electric power coming to the house overhead or underground? Where is the meter base and how big is it? If required, where will a temporary electrical meter base be located?
- Where is the electric panel box, sub panels: total number of circuits, free circuits, fuses or breakers, new or old style breakers? Locate and note condition.
- Is there access to running water? How is the water supplied—well or utility— where does it enter the building? Locate and note condition.
- Are there water issues around the foundation: does the grade slope away, does earth touch the siding, are there plants close to the building?
- Sewer line or septic system? Locate and note condition.

211 Generally a portable toilet is better for privacy and because it will be cleaned regularly.

- Is there an oil or propane tank or a gas meter? Locate and note condition.
- Cable-satellite? Locate and note condition.
- Is there a dog fence? Locate and note condition.
- Existing features—driveway, sidewalk, or landscaping—will they require protection? Note condition.
- Outbuildings: note condition. Will they affect work?
- Windows and doors: locations, sizes, condition?
- Exterior siding: trim, paint, finish, condition?
- Locate heat pump or air conditioning unit. Note condition.
- Roof style, pitch, overhang, soffit, roofing material, flashing, type of framing, gutters & downspouts, vents? Note condition.
- Chimney, flashing, cap? Note condition.

Inside building
- Interior wall coverings, trim, finish; note condition.
- Overall quality of painting, drywall finish, trim, doors & windows.
- Ceilings heights, skylights.
- Crawl space or basement access.
- Attic access. Vents in attic. Equipment in attic.
- Heating system, ducts, baseboard, radiators. Note age and condition.
- Fixtures, hardware. Note age and condition.
- Windows: height off the floor, height of ceiling, sizes, condition.
- Doors: location, sizes, condition.
- Wall & floor framing.
- Type of flooring, finishes. Note condition.
- Plumbing pipes, fixtures, hose bibs, water heater. Note condition.
- Closet locations, sizes, shelving, door style.
- Interior trim: baseboard, on doors & windows, crown, wainscoting.

SAMPLE, NEW HOME
CONSTRUCTION SCHEDULE

Pre-construction, 5%
- Zoning
- Site plan
- Utilities
- Engineer, layout
- Order roof trusses
- Permits
- Termite treatment

Excavation, footings, foundation, 10%
- Batter boards
- Excavation
- Plumb basement bath
- Footings
- Blocks, parge-block
- Waterproof block
- Well or city water connection
- Septic or sewer connection
- Driveway/walks
- Lay foundation PVC drain tile/gravel, filter paper
- Sill seal
- Lay plates/bolt down
- Order stairs
- Order exterior doors and windows
- Back fill / rough grade (after 1st floor deck framed)

Trusses, sheet roof, felt paper, 25%
- First floor system/joists, band, plywood
- Frame exterior walls system/first floor
- Second floor system/ joists, band, plywood
- Frame exterior wall system/ second floor
- Frame interior walls, blocking for drywall and cabinets

- Frame roof, felt, shingles
- Set exterior doors and windows
- Set stairs
- Brick veneer (siding if other than brick)
- Trades rough in; electrician, plumber, HVAC
- Fireplace
- Install interior doors
- Inspection: trades
- Inspection: framing
- Insulation
- Inspection: insulation
- Drywall hung

Drywall taped, 50%
- Trim: base, windows & doors, crown, chair rail, shelves, built-ins
- Set interior doors
- Stair railings
- Fireplace mantel
- Hardwood floors installed
- Hang garage door
- Gutters & downspouts
- Ceramic tile

Paint, first coat, 75%
- Caulk, putty, sand
- Touch up drywall
- Paint, second coat

Landscaping
- Grade & seed (sod)
- Cut grass / water lawn
- Kitchen cabinets
- Vanities
- Trades trim: electrician, plumber, HVAC, etc

- Finish floors: vinyl, carpet

Finish, 100%
- Remove materials and equipment
- Final cleanup
- Final punch-list

SAMPLE, DRAW SCHEDULE

Permits received 10%

Foundation 10%
- Footing foundations, walls, and piers installed
- Parge, foundation waterproofing, and drain tile installed
- Termite soil treatment, builders risk insurance

Roof sheathed 20%
- Floor joists and sub-flooring installed
- Exterior walls framed and partitions installed
- Roof framed, sheathed, and papered
- Exterior doors and windows installed
- Interior concrete completed

Ready for drywall 25%
- Plumbing rough-in
- HVAC rough-in
- Insulation (except blown in)
- Roof shingles installed

Ready to paint 25%
- Exterior trim, siding, and veneer
- Fireplace and chimney completed
- Drywall hung, taped, blocked, and finished
- Interior trim molding and door units installed

Completion 10%
- Well and septic and/or water/sewer connected
- Cabinets, vanities, and tops installed
- Floors and flooring coverings complete
- Plumbing fixtures, trim and hot water heater installed
- Electric fixtures and trim installed
- Furnace and appliances installed

- Painting complete
- Exterior walks and driveways installed
- Gutters and downspouts installed
- Final grading, seed/sod and landscaping installed
- Dwelling complete and ready for occupancy

SAMPLE, DRAW SCHEDULE

From:			
Client			
Builder:			
Job Address:			
Construction Progress	**Total %**	**%**	**Comments**
Foundation	14	14	
Frame	28	14	
Wall Sheathing	30	2	
Windows	32	2	
Cornice, Soffit	34	2	
Roof Covering	38	4	
Plumbing Rough	41	3	
Wiring Rough	44	3	
A/C Rough	47	3	
Brick/Stucco	54	7	
Sheetrock, wall insulation	60	6	
Int. Trim & Doors	65	5	
Cabinets	70	5	
Int. Paint	74	4	
Ceramic Tile	76	2	
Flooring - Tile/Wood	79	3	
Cabinet Tops	81	2	
Ext. Paint	83	2	
Electric Fixtures	85	2	
Plumbing Fixtures	87	2	
Drives and Walks	89	2	
Hardware	90	1	
Appliances	93	3	
Flooring - Carpet	95	2	
Compressor	96	1	
Landscape	98	2	
Punch-out	100	2	
% complete this period			
Total % complete			
Inspector's initials			
Date of inspection			

SAMPLE, SUBCONTRACTOR AGREEMENT

SUBCONTRACTOR TERMS

Project: client's name, address and contract information

Builder: builder's name, address and contract information

With the signature of the Subcontractor these two-pages of Subcontractor Terms becomes an addendum to the subcontractors' contract and the work to be done at the above address. These terms and the items detailed are legally binding and are included in the price of the contract provided by the Subcontractor.

The Subcontractor will obtain and pay for all permits and inspections as required by state and local codes. The Subcontractor is responsible for complying with all state and local codes. The Subcontractor is responsible for meeting the inspector on-site at the time of the inspection if someone must be present for the inspection.

The Subcontractor is to furnish and install all material (unless specifically excluded in their contract) and labor to provide a complete job. The Subcontractor agrees to provide all labor and material historically associated with his trade and not specifically detailed in the contract or on the plans. All work shall be neat, securely fastened, and shall meet or exceed accepted quality standards for this trade.

The Subcontractor will provide a schedule of when work will begin (start date to be coordinated with Builder), how many men will work throughout the project, and how long it will take to complete this work. The Subcontractor agrees to have sufficient materials, supplies, and personnel to meet the production schedule agreed to. The Subcontractor agrees to adjust his schedule to meet and work within the overall demands of the project.

The Subcontractor agrees to use the same lead workman or supervisor on the job from start to finish—including call backs—unless that person becomes ill or no longer works for the company.

The Subcontractor will include all sales tax in his price.

Builder may order changes to the work without invalidating this Subcontract. Any extra cost for changes must be documented in a change order and signed by (company rep) for Builder to be valid and none will be paid without a written and signed change order.

The Subcontractor will convey to his workmen that under no condition are his men to smoke in the building; not in the house, basement, attic, or garage. And, if his men smoke on-site outside the building, they will dispose of the butts in an appropriate place.

The Subcontractor will provide a per hour labor rate and a markup percentage on materials and these figures are to be used in all change orders or extra work. The Subcontractor agrees that, should change orders or extra work become necessary, this is the rate that will be charged throughout the project for all labor and material and that this rate and markup include all charges to the GC for extra work unless agreed in writing otherwise.

HOURLY RATE _____   MATERIAL MARKUP _____

The Subcontractor shall provide a current 'Certificate of Insurance' at the time the bid is submitted which specifies that the Builder will receive notice of cancellation or any change that occurs in the insurance coverage during the term of the project. Further, the Subcontractor agrees that until the Builder has a copy of a valid Certificate of Insurance issued by the Subcontractor's Insurance Company covering the items listed below that they will not be paid:

1. Liability insurance with a limit of one million dollars ($1,000,000.00) for each occurrence with a general aggregate of two million dollars ($2,000,000.00).

2. Agreement to indemnify and hold harmless the Builder for loss and any legal defense costs or that you add the Builder to your policy as an additional insured. One party will indemnify and hold harmless against claims or losses arising from the performance of the work of another party.

3. Workman's compensation insurance.

The Subcontractor agrees to keep the job site free of their trash and debris as the work progresses. The Subcontractor is responsible for placing all of their trash in an on-site dumpster (to be provided by Builder). Further, the Subcontractor agrees to leave the job site broom clean at the end of each workday. Should the Subcontractor fail to provide cleanup as outlined in this agreement, Builder, at its sole discretion, will have the cleanup done and deduct the cost from any amounts due the Subcontractor.

The Subcontractor agrees to be responsible for the security of their tools and materials that are left on-site.

The Subcontractor agrees to submit an invoice for each payment amount due. Payment will be made no later than fifteen (15) days after a correct invoice is received.

I understand and agree to the terms of this contract.

_____   _____
Subcontractor   Date

_____   _____
Company name

SAMPLE, SMALL JOB CONTRACT

Project: client's name, address and contract information

Builder: builder's name, address and contract information

We are pleased to provide the following contract and specifications for work to be done on your home. This contract comprises the entire agreement between the named parties.

SCOPE OF WORK

The work will take place in the library and will consist of the following:

Remove the existing paneling, two folding doors and casing, and the bay window casing. Protect the existing house with a barrier over the door opening.

Fur out the entire wall area, from floor to ceiling, with 1" × 3" furring strips and level those strips, making them straight and true. Install ¼" × 8' v-groove cherry paneling over the new furring strips. Fill all nail holes with colored putty and stain the paneling (color to be chosen).

Build approximately 36 lineal feet of adjustable shelving (use ½" KV track let into the uprights) from floor to ceiling, 9 ½" deep, with approximately 8'-6" of fixed single shelf over two doors & one bay window. All shelving, uprights, and horizontal pieces will be made of ¾" cherry veneer plywood. The face of the shelves and the uprights will be trimmed with solid cherry strips. The new shelving will be trimmed at the floor with quarter round stained material and at the ceiling with white painted pine crown molding. Fill all nail holes and stain all the wood (color to be chosen).

Trim the bay window with job milled solid cherry casing to be stained the same color as the bookcases.

The carpet will be cut back so that the bookcase rests on the concrete. The remaining carpet will be covered with ¼" hardboard during construction.

There is to be no work done on the ceiling, the fireplace, the steps, the floor (except to cut & protect the carpet) or the window (except trim).

There is no electrical work (except to put new plate covers on the existing switches and outlets), plumbing, or HVAC work included in this estimate.

Builder is to provide all of the materials and labor to complete this work as described.

Final cleanup to include removal of all job-related trash from the site & the reasonable cleaning of all new work and affected areas.

CONTRACT SUM

The Contract Sum for the described work is $14,500.00 (Fourteen Thousand and Five Hundred Dollars). The work consists solely of what is detailed in this contract. Extra work, added or made necessary by unforeseen circumstances, must be agreed to by both parties, and will be charged on a time and material basis at $35.00 per man hour, plus material, with 25% added onto the cost of all material.

PAYMENT

A 20% down payment shall be made the day the work begins. The balance of the contract will be paid as requested during the progress of the work with no less than 10% remaining at completion. Full payment shall be due & payable when the work is substantially completed.

The Owner(s) agree to pay a service charge of 1½% (one & one-half percent) per month on any payment more than 5 (five) days overdue & any legal or other fees incurred by Builder if it becomes necessary to collect past due payments.

BID CLARIFICATIONS

The Owner(s) is to provide access to toilet, electric power, & water on-site as well as garage space to be used as a workshop for the duration of this job.

ACCEPTANCE OF THIS PROPOSAL: I have read and understand the above listed price, specifications, and conditions. By signing this contract I agree to these terms and will abide by them. Builder is authorized to do this work as specified. Payment will be made as outlined above.

_____   _____

Owner   Owner

_____   _____

Date   Date

_____   _____

Builder   Date

SAMPLE, SMALL JOB CONTRACT TO DEVELOP JOB DOCUMENTS

Project: client's name, address and contract

Builder: builder's name, address and contract

AGREEMENT TO PROVIDE CONSTRUCTION SERVICES

THIS AGREEMENT becomes effective on the date of signing by (Client) and (Builder) and shall continue until termination in writing by either party or the work is complete. The Client resides at (client info)

BUILDER WILL provide construction services (drawings and specifications) at the rate of $00.00 per hour. Builder shall charge for all time related to this work, including, but not limited to, travel to and from the job, meetings, collecting information, phone calls, printing, mailing, making and revising drawings, writing and revising specifications, discussing the project with Clients and others. Builder will charge for miscellaneous items such as professional fees (if required), printing, and delivery services on each invoice.

THE FINAL COST to complete the design and specifications for this project, written or verbal, provided by Builder, and discussions of price between the Client and Builder are understood to be 'best judgment' only and are not in any way to be construed as assurances of the final cost of a project. (This can also be written as a fixed fee, if the cost is known.)

BUILDER SHALL invoice the Client weekly or at its discretion. The Client agrees to pay the Builder upon receipt of the invoice. The Client agrees to pay a service charge of two percent (2%) per month on any payment more than five (5) days overdue and any legal or other fees incurred if it becomes necessary to collect past due payments.

THIS CONTRACT contains the entire agreement of the named parties and there are no other promises or conditions in any other agreements, whether oral or written, unless this agreement is formally amended in writing and signed by both parties.

IF ANY PROVISION of this Agreement is held to be invalid or unenforceable for any reason, the remaining provisions shall continue to be valid and enforceable.

ACCEPTANCE OF PROPOSAL The above conditions are hereby accepted. Builder is authorized to do the work and bill as specified. Payment will be made as outlined above.

_____   _____

Client   date signed

_____   _____

Builder   date signed

SAMPLE, CHANGE ORDER

Change Order # 1

BUILDER

ADDRESS

PHONE

EMAIL / WEB SITE

:

Date: _____

Project name: _____

Project number _____

Original contract date _____

You are directed to make the following changes in this contract:
List each change order item with the cost

THANK YOU FOR THE WORK

The original contract sum was:	$ 0
Net amount of previous change orders:	$ 0
Total original contract amount plus or minus net change orders:	$ 0
Total amount of this change order:	$ 0
The new contract amount including this change order will be:	$ 0
The contract time will be changed by the following number of days:	(0) Days
The date of completion as of the date of this change order is:	n/a

Contractor: Owner:

                                     0

_____   _____

                                   Name

                                   0

_____   _____

                                   Address

_____   _____

               estimator   Signature: Date

_____   _____

Signature: Date   Signature: Date

SAMPLE, CONSTRUCTION INDEX,
headings, sub-headings, line items[212]

Di	Sub	Tag	Item Code	Description	Alt. UofM	UofM	Material	Labor	SubC	Other	Hours
06				Floor Framing							
06	070			Wood Foundations							
06	070	☐	06.000.	2" x 4" & 1/2" wood foundation		SF	4.70	2.90		0.00	0.064
06	070	☐	06.001.	2" x 6" & 1/2" wood foundation		SF	6.77	3.14		0.00	0.069
06	070	☐	06.002.	2" x 8" & 3/4" wood foundation		SF	7.93	3.47		0.00	0.076
06	075			Beams & Columns							
06	075	☐	06.100.	W8 x 13 steel beam		LF	8.35	7.45		0.00	0.184
06	075	☐	06.101.	W8 x 17 steel beam		LF	10.90	7.45		0.00	0.164
06	075	☐	06.110.	4" x 8" wood beam		LF	2.83	2.86		0.00	0.063
06	075	☐	06.111.	4" x 10" wood beam		LF	3.69	3.67		0.00	0.081
06	075	☐	06.112.	4" x 12" wood beam		LF	4.43	4.28		0.00	0.094
06	075	☐	06.113.	6" x 8" wood beam		LF	4.18	3.89		0.00	0.085
06	075	☐	06.114.	6" x 10" wood beam		LF	5.54	4.90		0.00	0.108
06	075	☐	06.130.	Flitch plate		LF	16.52	11.83		0.00	0.260
06	075	☐	06.135.	Flitch plate		LF	4.54	8.57		0.00	0.189
06	075	☐	06.136.	Flitch plate		LF	5.33	8.98		0.00	0.198
06	075	☐	06.210.	Steel column 3-1/2" Diameter 8'-0"H		EA	64.90	24.48		0.00	0.539
06	075	☐	06.211.	Steel column 3-1/2" Diameter 9'-0"H		EA	71.98	24.48		0.00	0.539
06	075	☐	06.212.	Steel column 3-1/2" Diameter 10'-0"H		EA	79.06	24.48		0.00	0.539
06	080			Floor Framing							
06	080	☐	06.300.	2" x 4" mudsill		LF	1.29	1.00		0.00	0.022
06	080	☐	06.301.	2" x 6" mudsill		LF	1.57	1.10		0.00	0.024
06	080	☐	06.302.	2" x 8" mudsill		LF	1.86	1.16		0.00	0.026
06	080	☐	06.303.	4" x 6" mudsill		LF	2.45	1.75		0.00	0.039
06	080	☐	06.304.	4" x 8" mudsill		LF	3.08	1.84		0.00	0.040
06	080	☐	06.310.	2" x 4" redwood mudsill		LF	1.94	1.26		0.00	0.028
06	080	☐	06.311.	2" x 6" redwood mudsill		LF	2.32	1.37		0.00	0.030
06	080	☐	06.320.	16" OC 1" x 4" sleepers		SF	0.49	1.16		0.00	0.026
06	080	☐	06.321.	16" OC 2" x 3" sleepers		SF	0.64	1.26		0.00	0.028
06	080	☐	06.322.	16" OC 2" x 4" sleepers		SF	0.77	1.29		0.00	0.028
06	080	☐	06.323.	16" OC 2" x 6" sleepers		SF	1.01	1.31		0.00	0.029
06	080	☐	06.324.	24" OC 1" x 4" sleepers		SF	0.38	0.84		0.00	0.018
06	080	☐	06.325.	24" OC 2" x 3" sleepers		SF	0.46	0.90		0.00	0.020
06	080	☐	06.326.	24" OC 2" x 4" sleepers		SF	0.55	0.92		0.00	0.020
06	080	☐	06.327.	24" OC 2" x 6" sleepers		SF	0.73	0.94		0.00	0.021
06	080	☐	06.330.	16" OC 2" x 6" floor joists		SF	0.64	1.00		0.00	0.022
06	080	☐	06.331.	16" OC 2" x 8" floor joists		SF	0.86	1.06		0.00	0.023
06	080	☐	06.332.	16" OC 2" x 10" floor joists		SF	1.23	1.12		0.00	0.025
06	080	☐	06.333.	16" OC 2" x 12" floor joists		SF	1.54	1.16		0.00	0.026
06	080	☐	06.334.	24" OC 2" x 6" floor joists		SF	0.44	0.82		0.00	0.018
06	080	☐	06.335.	24" OC 2" x 8" floor joists		SF	0.61	0.86		0.00	0.019
06	080	☐	06.336.	24" OC 2" x 10" floor joists		SF	0.86	0.90		0.00	0.020
06	080	☐	06.337.	24" OC 2" x 12" floor joists		SF	1.07	0.94		0.00	0.021
06	080	☐	06.340.	12" OC 9-1/2" wood I-joists		SF	1.80	1.45		0.00	0.032
06	080	☐	06.341.	12" OC 11-7/8" wood I-joists		SF	1.94	1.53		0.00	0.034
06	080	☐	06.342.	12" OC 14" wood I-joists		SF	2.80	1.61		0.00	0.035
06	080	☐	06.343.	12" OC 16" wood I-joists		SF	3.13	1.63		0.00	0.036
06	080	☐	06.344.	16" OC 9-1/2" wood I-joists		SF	1.40	1.14		0.00	0.025
06	080	☐	06.345.	16" OC 11-7/8" wood I-joists		SF	1.49	1.22		0.00	0.027

12 Screen shot from HomeTech Advantage estimating program.

SAMPLE, PREQUALIFYING
CLIENT PHONE INTERVIEW

When conducting phone interviews, be friendly and inquisitive and listen more than you talk. You are not selling at this point; you are trying to determine if these potential clients are a good fit for your company. When you decide, schedule an appointment or let them know that the work is not for you. If you decline their work, always be friendly and, if possible, refer them to someone who might fit their needs better. Modify this list to make it meaningful to your company.

- Where did you get our name and what can we do for you?

    - A referral requires the most attention and is more likely to turn into a job.

    - A cold call will require more scrutiny and more selling if you decide it is a job that you want.

- Ask them to explain the scope of work, or as much as they know of it.

- Ask questions to flesh out the work so that you can better understand what they are looking for.

- Do they have a budget? If they don't or they don't want to tell you what it is, get a range. A bathroom renovation costs from five to fifty thousand dollars, where are they on this scale?

- When do they expect to begin work? How long do they expect it to take?

- Who are the decision maker(s), what is their relationship?

- If you make an appointment, try to meet with all of the decision makers at once.

- Do they have job documents? If so who created them? Are they planning to use them as they now exist or are they going to change them? If they are to be changed, who will do that and what is the timeline?

- Do they dwell more on what it will cost or the design/result, that is, are they more interested in price or quality and organization?

- Do they need design–build services or are they looking for bidders?

- How many estimates are they getting?

  - Do they have a contractor that they favor?

  - If so, why are they looking for other prices?

  - If they are trying to check prices, if it interests you, offer to do an estimate for a fee.

- Have they built before? Ask them to talk about that experience.

SAMPLE, IN-PERSON CLIENT INTERVIEW

Some questions are not meant to be asked directly but intuited through listening and observation. At the first interview, listen more than you talk. Modify this list to make it meaningful to your company.

Ask:

- Ask them to explain their project in detail, drilling into some of the larger questions or thorny issues as seems appropriate.

- Walk around the site or building with them and have them talk about what they have in mind.

- Determine if planning and job documents are required and determine who will provide these.

- Discuss their budget and their expectations around that figure.

- Have they done other projects, ask them to talk about those in some detail.

    - Who did the work? Why aren't they using them again?

    - Were they happy with the project?

    - What lessons did they learn?

    - What will their main concerns be this time?

- What are their main concerns about this project?

- Begin to explain how you work and what you can do for them.

Notice:

- Are they direct, clear, reasonable, and honest?

- Do they answer questions and make decisions easily?

- Are there hard edges or issues you can't understand?

- Are they overly concerned with cost, being ripped off?

- Are they know-it-alls? Are they demanding or pushy?

- Is something not being said? If so, ask that question.

- Are they treating each other and you with respect?

- Are they (all) genuinely interested in the project?

- Are they realistic about what they want done, the cost, and the time frame?

- What are their main concerns? That is, what points do they keep coming back to: cost, service, speed, quality, design?

BIBLIOGRAPHY

This bibliography contains some items I have used for years and others that are fairly new. Some of the older ones may be hard to find: try used bookstores, the out-of-print market on the web, and Google Books. This is not a comprehensive list and there exist many excellent books, websites, catalogs, and references to be discovered. That said, a significant percentage of the information sold about residential construction offers little more than warmed-over facts, simplistic ideas, or inaccurate information, and thus it requires discrimination and effort not to waste your money and time on the rubbish.

> "When you first start to study a field, it seems like you have to memorize a zillion things. You don't. What you need is to identify the core principles—generally three to twelve of them that govern the field. The million things you thought you had to memorize are simply various combinations of the core principles."
> —John Reed

GENERAL CONSTRUCTION

A Practical Guide to Building Construction, Edgar Lion, Prentice-Hall, 1980, good general reading for a primer of the entire field with good descriptions of materials and methods of construction.

Blueprint Reading for the Building Trades, John E. Traister, Craftsman Book Company, 1981.

The National Association of Home Builders (NAHB) produces books and software for the residential construction industry.

Construction: Materials, Methods, Careers, Jack M. Landers, Goodheart-Willcox Publisher, 1983, a good introduction to the entire field of building. It uses many photographs and details the items indicated in the title. The descriptions are brief and clear.

Dwelling House Construction, Albert G. H. Dietz, MIT Press, 1991, a residential classic that should be read and referred to often.

House, Tracy Kidder, Houghton Mifflin Company, 1999, an excellent description of the relationship between homeowner, architect, and builder. It accurately describes the rewards and frustrations of being a builder and it makes good light reading.

Fine Home Building / Taunton Press publish books for the residential construction industry.[213]

The Well-Built House, Jim Locke, Houghton Mifflin Company, 1992, in an ideal world every builder and customer would read this book. It contains useful information about the interaction of the builder/ homeowner/ designer.

ESTIMATING

Craftsman Book Company publishes construction books of all kinds, including estimating data and software. I have no experience with their product.[214]

Remodeling & Renovation Cost Estimator by HomeTech Publishing is an excellent cost book and software product, both because it concentrates exclusively on residential work and because of its layout. Toward the beginning of the printed book, there is a description of why bidding high enough is so important; read it carefully. I have always found HomeTech's cost estimates to be high— high is better than low—but as with all such products it will become more accurate and thus more valuable the longer you use it.[215]

13 https://www.Tauntonstore.com/homebuilding.html

14 http://craftsman-book.com/products

15 https://www.hometechpublishing.com

Means Estimating Handbook, Reed Construction Data, current edition. The older version of the copy that I owned was primarily concerned with commercial building so it may not be worth buying for a residential builder; however, if you can find one in a library, a used book store, or from a friend, read the Introduction, Division 1, and study the "13 general rules of estimating." Means has several versions and formats for their estimating data, although I never had any luck using their estimating products for residential construction. Means publishes construction books of all types.[216]

National Construction Estimator 2013, Richard Pray, Craftsman Books Company.

National Repair & Remodeling Estimator 2013, Albert S. Paxton, Craftsman Book Company.

Professional Cost Estimating, Walt Stoeppelwerth, HomeTech Information Systems, 1990. Walt was a clear, firm voice in the discussion of charging enough for the services you provide.

Remodelers Handbook: A Manual of Professional Practice for Home Improvement Contractors, Benjamin Williams, Craftsman Books Company, 1976.

Walker's Building Estimator's Reference Book, Frank Walker, Frank R. Walker Company, 2006, a good source of information, but like many books, it tries to cover the entire industry, from high-rise buildings to remodeling. For this reason, I believe that it has less value to a residential builder than books focused exclusively on residential work. If you can find it at the local library or from a friend, it is worth reading the first few chapters and reviewing the lists and charts, which can be helpful.

216 https://rsmeans.reedconstructiondata.com

CONSTRUCTION REFERENCES

Black's Law Dictionary, Garner, Newman, Jackson, McDaniel, West Group, 2011, with brief clear definitions, this is an excellent source of information about legal terms and concepts.

Smith, Currie & Hancock's Common Sense Construction Law, A Practical Guide for the Construction Professional, Thomas J. Kelleher Jr. and G. Scott Walters, John Wiley & Sons, 2009, a practical summary of legal issues facing builders. It will help to have this book at hand when writing contracts or to better understand a legal issue when dealing with a difficult subcontractor or customer.

Olin's Construction: Principles, Materials and Methods, H. Leslie Simmons, John Wiley & Sons, 2011, a huge book providing fascinating and in-depth details about nearly every area of construction. The information is primarily written with some illustrations. If you own the book and review items with which you are about to work, over time, you will learn valuable construction facts.

JLC Field Guides, A Manual of Best Practice, Volumes 1 & 2, DeKorne, Healey, Vitullo, Journal of Light Construction, 2005, likely the best source for residential construction details available as of this writing.

The Anatomy of a House, **A Picture Dictionary of Architectural and Design Elements,** Fayal Greene, Doubleday, current version, a small book with clear easy access to the information.

The Architect's Portable Handbook, First-Step Rules of Thumb for Building Design, John Guthrie, McGraw-Hill Portable Handbook, 2010, as noted in its introduction "it compacts 20% of the data that is needed 80% of the time…" and does it well. It is a book that one can both study and refer to for years.

Residential & Light Commercial Construction Standards,
Donald Reynolds, RS Means, 2002, an excellent source for
residential construction details. It is made up primarily of drawings
with some text. You will learn a great deal browsing through it.

Wikipedia is a good place to gain a broad understanding of
specific building topics.

CONSTRUCTION STANDARDS, INDEXES, SPECIFICATIONS, AND CODES

Architectural Woodworking Quality Standards, Architectural
Woodwork Institute, 1978.

Architectural Graphic Standards For Residential Construction,
Nina M. Giglio, John Wiley & Sons, 2010. This is an expensive
book and its main focus is designers/architects. But, because
in many ways it is the standard for the residential construction
industry, I recommend that you buy it, study it, and refer to it
often.

Code Check, various authors, Taunton Press, current version
of each version. There are several different Code Check books—
the original, electrical, building, plumbing & mechanical, and
commercial—and they offer the clearest, most logical presentation
of code requirements that I'm aware of.

Construction Specifications Writing: Principles and Procedures,
Kalin, Weygant, Rosen, and Regener, John Wiley & Sons, 2010.

International Code Council publishes code-related books and
materials. Search its site to find the code book(s) that apply to the
type of work you do and the area of the country that you work in.

National Association of Home Builders (NAHB) publishes
various construction codes and standards.[217]

---

217 https://www.nahb.org

The CSI Construction Specifications Practice Guide, The Construction Specifications Institute, John Wiley & Sons, 2011.

Occupational Safety and Health Administration (OSHA) produces several books detailing its standards and regulations, including *Standards for the Construction Industry.*[218]

Quality Standards for the Professional Remodeler, National Association of Home Builders, Remodelers Council, 1991.

MAGAZINES & PERIODICALS:

Fine Home Building (FHB), a monthly magazine with exceptional photographs and excellent articles on residential construction. Its website has useful links and videos as well as providing access to the most recent magazines. FHB also offers a searchable CD that includes all past issues; this is an extraordinary resource. FHB is the best residential construction magazine available today, although it offers limited information about business management.[219]

The Journal of Light Construction (JLC), a monthly trade magazine, is a good source for residential construction information. One of their most valuable products is the *JLC Archives*, which offers every article and photograph from every past issue in an easily searchable format. They have many good business management articles.[220] JLC is published by Hanley Wood, LLC.

Builder, The Magazine of the National Association of Home Builders, is a free monthly magazine with a huge number of advertisements and some very good articles. Builder is published by Hanley Wood, LLC.[221]

---

18 https://www.osha.gov/pls/publications/publication.html
19 http://www.finehomebuilding.com/
20 http://www.jlconline.com/
21 http://www.builderonline.com/

INSPIRATIONAL BUSINESS BOOKS

Built to Last, Jim Collins and Jerry I. Porras, HarperCollins Books, 1997.

Good to Great, Jim Collins, HarperCollins Books, 2001.

Principle-Centered Leadership, Stephen R. Covey, Simon & Schuster, 1991.

The Seven Habits of Highly Effective People, Stephen R. Covey, Simon & Schuster, 2004.[222]

PRINTED FORMS

Associated General Contractors of America, Inc. (AGC)

New England Business Systems (NEBS) 1-800-225-9540. These folks sell business forms. They have good quality, basic, cost effective forms for almost anything a new builder needs.

Stationery stores often sell basic contracts and other business forms.

CATALOGS

Garrett Wade Tool Catalog, 800-221-2942, www.garrettwade.com

Grainger Catalog, 1-800-473-3473, www.grainger.com. This is a huge catalog, which lists and has drawings of thousands of tools and supplies. It is published once a year and can be ordered or picked up at a Grainger store for free, and the full catalog is also online. The catalog has a complete list of store locations. It is good place to buy tools and equipment and also to learn what is available.

---

222 Stephen R. Covey's website is worth a visit: https://www.stephencovey.com/7habits/7habits.php

INDEX

Page numbers followed by n indicate footnote., ,

QUOTATIONS FROM...

THE
ELEMENTS
OF
BUILDING

A Business Handbook For
Residential Builders & Tradesmen

You may order this book on line with a credit card
at www.elements-of-building.com, or, you may send
a check for $44.00 ($37.00 + $7.00 for shipping)
made out to *Mark Q. Kerson* and mailed to:

EOB
3650 Chambers Street
Eugene, OR 97405

When your check clears our bank we will immediately
mail your book. Be sure to include a mailing
address, e-mail address, and phone number.

The author appreciates readers thoughts and
comments. Please use this e-mail address to contact him:
EOB@DPLUS.NET

Made in United States
Troutdale, OR
12/05/2023

15407442R00219